Twayne's New Critical Introductions to
Shakespeare

CORIOLANUS

By the same author

Gissing in Context (London: Macmillan, 1975)
Tragedy: Shakespeare and the Greek Example (Oxford: Blackwell, 1987)

Twayne's New Critical Introductions to Shakespeare

CORIOLANUS

Adrian Poole

University Lecturer in English and Fellow of
Trinity College, Cambridge

TWAYNE PUBLISHERS · BOSTON
A Division of G. K. Hall & Co.

Published in the United States by Twayne Publishers,
division of G. K. Hall & Co.,
70 Lincoln Street, Boston, Massachusetts.

Published simultaneously in Great Britain by
Havester · Wheatsheaf
66 Wood Lane End, Hemel Hempstead,
Hertfordshire HP24RG.

Library of Congress Cataloging-in-Publication Data
Poole, Adrian.
  Coriolanus / Adrian Poole.
    p. cm. — (Twayne's new critical introductions to
Shakespeare)
  Bibliography: p.
  Includes index.
  ISBN 0-8057-8709-7.   ISBN 0-8057-8713-5 (pbk.)
  1. Shakespeare, William, 1564–1616. Coriolanus. I. Title.
II. Series.
PR2805.P6 1988
822.3'3—dc19   88-18051
                                                          CIP

To
Theodore Redpath
and
Leo Salingar

Titles in the Series

GENERAL EDITOR: GRAHAM BRADSHAW

Jane Adamson	*Troilus and Cressida*
Graham Bradshaw	*Henry IV*
Maurice Charney	*Titus Andronicus*
S. L. Goldberg	*Antony and Cleopatra*
Harriett Hawkins	*Measure for Measure*
Alexander Leggatt	*King Lear*
Michael Long	*Macbeth*
John Lyon	*The Merchant of Venice*
Tom McCavera	*The Tempest*
A. D. Nuttall	*Timon of Athens*
Adrian Poole	*Coriolanus*
Wilbur Sanders	*The Winter's Tale*
Cedric Watts	*Hamlet*
Sheldon Zitner	*All's Well That Ends Well*

General Editor's Preface

The *Harvester New Critical Introductions to Shakespeare* series will include studies of all Shakespeare's plays, together with two volumes on the non-dramatic verse, and is designed to offer a challenge to all students of Shakespeare.

Each volume will be brief enough to read in an evening, but long enough to avoid those constraints which are inevitable in articles and short essays. Each contributor will develop a sustained critical reading of the play in question, which addresses those difficulties and critical disagreements which each play has generated.

Different plays present different problems, different challenges and excitements. In isolating these, each volume will present a preliminary survey of the play's stage history and critical reception. The volumes then provide a more extended discussion of these matters in the main text, and of matters relating to genre, textual problems and the use of source material, or to historical and theoretical issues. But here, rather than setting a row of dragons at the gate, we have assumed that 'background' should figure only as it emerges into a critical foreground; part of the critical endeavour is to establish, and sift, those issues which seem most pressing.

So, for example, when Shakespeare determined that *his* Othello and Desdemona should have no time to live together, or that Cordelia dies while Hermione survives, his deliberate departures from his source material have a critical significance which is often blurred, when discussed in the context of lengthily detailed surveys of 'the sources'. Alternatively, plays like *The Merchant of Venice* or *Measure for Measure* show Shakespeare welding together different 'stories' from quite different sources, so that their relation to each other becomes a matter for critical debate. And Shakespeare's dramatic practice poses different critical questions when we ask—or if we ask: few do—why particular characters in a poetic drama speak only in verse or only in prose; or when we try to engage with those recent, dauntingly specialised and controversial textual studies which set out to establish the evidence for authorial revisions or joint authorship. We all read *King Lear* and *Macbeth*, but we are not all textual critics; nor are textual critics always able to show where their arguments have critical consequences which concern us all.

Just as we are not all textual critics, we are not all linguists, cultural anthropologists, psychoanalysts or New Historicists. The diversity of contemporary approaches to Shakespeare is unprecedented, enriching, bewildering. One aim of this series is to represent what is illuminating in this diversity. As the hastiest glance through the list of contributors will confirm, the series does not attempt to 're-read' Shakespeare by placing an ideological grid over the text and reporting on whatever shows through. Nor would the series' contributors always agree with each other's arguments, or premises; but each has been invited to develop a sustained critical argument which will also provide its own critical and historical context—by taking account of those issues which have perplexed or divided audiences, readers, and critics past and present.

Graham Bradshaw

Contents

Preface   xi

Acknowledgements   xiv

The Stage History   xv

The Critical Reception   xvii

1.   'You shames of Rome!'   1

2.   'Acclamations hyperbolical'   23

3.   'Most sweet voices!'   47

4.   'O world, thy slippery turns!'   74

5.   'O mother, mother!'   96

Notes   122

Bibliography   133

Index   138

Preface

In 1959 Laurence Olivier played the title role of *Coriolanus* for the second time in his career. A responsive theatre critic records the following impression that Olivier made at a famously climactic moment:

> The *fortissimo* he gave to 'Alone I did it, Boy' left one in no state to speculate about the accuracy of the taunt which aroused it. Olivier may have been subjecting Marcius to one of the shocks of recognition he likes to inflict on an audience. But one cannot experience one shock and assess another at the same time. The audience quivered at the sound of Olivier's voice like Avon swans at a sudden crack of thunder.[1]

There are no swans in *Coriolanus* itself but there are geese, and the shock that Kitchin imagines Olivier giving an audience repeats the shocking effect that Martius has on his fellow beings within the play. He makes them flinch and shrink and cower: he *hurts*. Of another of Olivier's great moments, Kitchin writes, 'the speech had an impact like jagged stones'.[2]

Kitchin's vivid impressions suggest one of the major difficulties and interests in this great, brutal play. No other play of Shakespeare's is dominated to the same extent by the brute physical presence of the central character, the very sight and sound of the man. He epitomises the physical impact of the play as a whole, which assaults and excites the eye and ear more violently than any other play of Shakespeare's maturity. It is certainly his noisiest play, but it is also one in which the range of noise, and the range of its relations to actions and feelings, are of peculiar importance. The 'sight-and-sound' of all of Shakespeare's plays is an essential ingredient which literary criticism often fails to allow for, but here it poses a particularly vital challenge. Many critics have written about the play as if their withers had never been wrung by a fine performance in the theatre. And to succeed on the stage, nothing less will do than a 'Coriolanus' who can inspire something comparable in the audience to what he inspires in the other characters on stage.

Our experience of a Shakespeare play does not begin and end with a single reading or the witnessing of a single performance. We collect ourselves both during and after the reading and the witnessing, but at some level we recognise an untapped potential for future thoughts and ideas and feelings, both in ourselves and in the text. Literary criticism is often prone to a conclusiveness that seeks to cut off the future life of the text. This is particularly calamitous when the text in question appeals for a future life in the successive recreations of dramatic performance. Yet although Shakespearian tragedies present experiences sufficiently shocking that readers and audiences are understandably keen to seek refuge in their own conclusions, we can usually be lured back by the prospect of imagining it again. This time it will be different.

Coriolanus is not unique amongst Shakespearian tragedies, but it does focus with a peculiar intensity on the gap between our experiences of the play and the conclusions we reach about them. It is easier to reach conclusions in the cool solitude of reading than in the heated, collective milieu of theatrical performance. Before passing judgement on the play's central character, his personal and political immaturity, his woefully inadequate grasp of language, his deplorable manners and hateful class-hatred, it is necessary to realise the sheer danger of his presence. Our experience of the play is not confined to the theatre; we think and judge in the theatre and we feel and imagine in the study. This play makes it our business to think about our need to reach conclusions. It does this by exposing to our view the workings of this need in the characters on stage. But it also subjects us to powerful shocks such as prompt this need in ourselves.

I have tried to offer a close reading of the play that stays alive both to the impact of the text and to the ideas on which it draws and to which it can lead. My reading follows the play's own movement through time in words and actions, pausing now and then to consider some of the more general issues that the play raises. The chapters take their headings from five brief utterances of the central character that I take to mark significant phases of the play. It is not coincidental that four of them are exclamations, while the fifth refers to the 'acclamations' of others. As a sequence, they chart in miniature what seems to me the inner movement of the play.

Acknowledgements

Unless otherwise stated, all quotations from *Coriolanus* follow the text of the New Arden Shakespeare edition, ed. Philip Brockbank (London: Methuen, 1976), to which all references by Act, scene and line also relate. All other references to and quotations from Shakespeare follow the Alexander Text: *William Shakespeare: The Complete Works*, ed. Peter Alexander (London and Glasgow: Collins, 1951).

The Stage History

It would be surprising if a play so vividly conceived for the theatre had not been performed in Shakespeare's lifetime, but in fact no direct evidence of a production has survived.

Until Macready began his series of productions in 1819, the history of Shakespeare's play on the stage is complicated by the adaptations of Nahum Tate (*The Ingratitude of a Common-Wealth*, probably first performed in 1681 and published in 1682), and John Dennis (*The Invader of His Country: or, The Fatal Resentment*, first performed in 1719 and published in 1720), and by the independent version penned by James Thomson and performed after his death in 1749. For the next fifty years or so Thomson and Shakespeare became unwitting collaborators in the hybrid versions that dominated the London stage as *Coriolanus: or the Roman Matron*, first in the adaptation credited to Thomas Sheridan and then through John Philip Kemble's celebrated series of productions, from 1789 to 1797 and again from 1806 to 1817. Both Garrick before Kemble and Kean after him attempted uncontaminated versions of Shakespeare's play, but with relatively little success.

From Macready onwards, Shakespeare's text has shrugged off overt adaptation, though it is worth noting an unfinished German version by Brecht, which after his death became the basis for a production by the Berliner Ensemble.

Yet no matter how ostensibly faithful to 'the original', all
theatrical performance in effect involves revision or
reinterpretation. In my account of the play I shall examine
the points in the text that especially warrant and demand the
interpretation of actors and audience.

The play's central role appealed to all the great actor-
managers, to Garrick, Kemble, Kean, Macready, Phelps and
Irving, and in the last fifty years the English stage has seen
some notable performances by Laurence Olivier (1938 and
1959), John Clements (1948), Anthony Quayle (1952),
Richard Burton (1953–4), John Neville (1963), Nicol
Williamson (1973), Alan Howard (1977–9) and Ian
McKellen (1984–5). There have been some memorable
Volumnias, including Sarah Siddons, Sybil Thorndike,
Edith Evans and, more recently, Irene Worth. Less
frequently a Menenius has lingered in the public
imagination (such as Alec Guinness's at the Old Vic in 1948)
and an Aufidius (such as Ian McKellen's in Tyrone
Guthrie's 1963 Nottingham production). The play lends
itself to spectacle and it has enjoyed some famously
colourful and noisy revivals, from the 1754–5 hybrid at
Covent Garden with its staggering Roman Ovation
(flamens, lictors, incense-bearers, captive generals in chains,
the lot), to Peter Hall's ear-splitting 1984–5 National
Theatre production. The play's stage history bears out its
peculiarly demanding and appealing character, in that like
Shakespeare's other great Roman tragedy, *Antony and
Cleopatra*, it requires both massive command of violent
sound and large movement,and also great delicacy in the
handling of minute detail. It demands both ostentation and
reticence.

For a selection of more detailed accounts of some of the
play's vicissitudes in the theatre, the reader is referred to the
following: Ralph Berry, 'The Metamorphoses of
Coriolanus', *Shakespeare Quarterly* 26 (1975), pp. 172–83;
Philip Brockbank's introduction to his Arden edition of the
play, pp. 71–89; David Daniell, *'Coriolanus' in Europe*,

London: Athlone Press, 1980; Laurence Kitchin, *Mid-Century Drama*, London: Faber & Faber, 1960, pp. 143–9; J. R. Mulryne, '*Coriolanus* at Stratford-upon-Avon: Three Actors' Remarks', *Shakespeare Quarterly* 29 (1978), pp. 323–32; G. C. D. Odell, *Shakespeare from Betterton to Irving*, 2 vols, London: Constable & Co., 1921; Kenneth Tynan, *Tynan on Theatre*, Harmondsworth: Penguin, 1964, pp. 94–6.

The Critical Reception

The issues that have come to seem most important in critical accounts of the play may be grouped under three broad headings: politics, character and language. The most valuable readings of the play bring out the interrelationships between these three elements.

Coleridge believed that the play demonstrated 'the wonderful philosophic impartiality in Shakespeare's politics'. This is a blithe conclusion. Coleridge's younger contemporary Hazlitt saw the play as confirming the imagination's appalling partiality to the glamour of political power. Most critics have had something to say about the antagonistic political principles apparently embodied in the figures of Caius Martius and 'the people'. In recent years, for example, Littlewood and Vickers have voiced support for what they see in Martius as an authentic political idealism and integrity; others such as Barton and Dollimore have argued that 'the people' are represented more sympathetically than has often been realised. Several critics have written well on the ethical and psychological aspects of the play's politics, particularly as these are focused in the Roman ideas of honour and valour. There are valuable essays on this topic by Gordon and Rabkin, and Bamber and Kahn both link the play interestingly to *Macbeth* in the course of examining Shakespeare's representation of an ethos of manliness. Much useful work has been done on the role played by Roman history in the imagination of Shakespeare and his contemporaries, and also more specifically on the ways in which this play may be supposed to have engaged with the political discourse of the early years of James I's reign. Particularly important in these respects are the items listed in the bibliography by Barton, Brower, Cantor, Gordon, Huffman, Miola, Simmons and Zeefeld.

The play dramatises some difficult questions about the relation between 'character' and 'politics', but many readings present the play's politics as eventually subordinate to 'character'. Rabkin, for example, concludes that through his supposedly political behaviour Martius demonstrates 'the priority of personality to principle'. Some of the most important arguments about the play revolve around the problem of Martius's personality. Bradley believed that at the climax of the play Martius saves his soul. (On the question of what Shakespeare and his contemporaries may have felt about the soul of a pagan such as Martius, Simmond's arguments command attention.) But many modern readers doubt whether Martius can even be justly said to have a self to be saved, let alone a soul. There are those such as Dollimore who contend that the play dismembers the very idea of an intrinsic, autonomous self. At a milder level, several critics express disappointment at Martius's failure to discover in himself as vital an inner life as other Shakespearian tragic characters; Cantor, Danson and Stockholder, for example, take this line. Sanders on the other hand argues for the existence of a rich inwardness in Martius, and with others he points to the recalcitrant reticence not only of the central character but also of the form and manner of the play as a whole. From another angle, Goldman has a good essay on the ways in which 'character' is something created and perceived in the movement of the play itself.

The third main area of critical interest concerns the

language of the play, and the role of language *in* the play. Some of its most distinctive stylistic features, of imagery and syntax and rhetorical figure, have been ably studied by Charney, Danson, Doran, Goldman, Paster and Wilson Knight. But to a number of recent critics the play has seemed so purposively to foreground the ways in which language creates ideas of personal and political identity as to become the central subject of the play itself. Fish, for example, goes so far as to say that the play is 'about' speech-act theory. Calderwood, Danson, Dollimore, Goldman, Sicherman and Van Dyke have all written helpfully about the play's concern with the extent and limits of language's power to persuade and express and interpret.

In my own account of the play I shall be showing in some detail how the text promotes these different kinds of attention and disagreement, and I shall dwell on the most important general arguments as the dramatic situation brings them into focus. I shall stress the diversity of potentialities inherent in the text. It is this diversity that ensures the continued vitality of the play, its availability for repeated recreation by readers, critics, directors and actors. A literary text, and above all a dramatic text, contains all its own future possibilities latent within it, but these have to be recreated by the active engagement of readers and actors. This does not mean that we should ignore the historical distance between ourselves and the circumstances of a text's first production. What it means is that reading is or should be an essentially comparative activity, and that it is through this activity that we find substance in the idea of reappropriating history.

·1·

'You shames of Rome!'

Coriolanus begins with a rush. The stage is instantly filled with physical tumult. There is a menace in the start of many Shakespeare plays, but nowhere is it as overt and palpable as this. These people are intent on violence, ready to die and ready to kill.

It is a well-known fact that like all good citizens Shakespeare hated mobs. Most literary critics are good citizens and therefore disposed to bring the following agreed truths to bear on this play: 'We know that Shakespeare detested the city mob';[1] 'The populace is consistently presented as unstable, fickle, anarchical, deficient in vision';[2] 'Shakespeare portrays the unreasoning violence of mob action'.[3] But surprising as it may be, we know nothing for certain of Shakespeare's feelings about city mobs, the populace in this play is not consistently presented as anarchical, and their violence is not unreasoning.[4]

'Reasoning' is exactly what these people engage in, albeit abrupt, nervous, precipitate. 'Think how reluctantly men decide to revolt!' remarks one of the speakers in Brecht's study of the play's first scene.[5] To call them a 'mob' is already to solve a problem which will be one of the play's main subjects. Does what you call people make them what they are? In fact we never hear the word 'mob' in Shakespeare or anywhere else until the *mobile vulgus* is

1

vernacularised later in the seventeenth century. The play's
opening stage-direction describes them as 'a Company of
Mutinous Citizens', and a later one will call for a 'rabble'
(III.i.179, 261). In its small way this calls attention to the
difficulty of choosing a word to describe such congregations
of men in the mass. We will hear many attempts to concert
agreement about this human multitude. In the first scene
alone we hear them addressed or referred to as 'good
citizens', 'mine honest neighbours', 'mutinous members',
'rats', 'dissentious rogues', 'curs', 'the rabble', 'fragments',
'worshipful mutiners' and 'the people'. As the play
progresses the tribunes will relentlessly trumpet the call of
'the people', while their chief enemy will snarl with
ingenious ferocity at 'Hydra here', 'this bosom multiplied',
and 'the beast with many heads'.

Before these mutinous citizens can confront their chief
enemy, they are checked by a patrician who represents one
aspect of what they are up against in the power of words.
They find it difficult utterly to mistrust Menenius Agrippa.
How resolved are they? Nothing could be as resolved as the
image of passionless implacability with which Menenius
seeks to cow them in his first extended speech:

> you may as well
> Strike at the heaven with your staves, as lift them
> Against the Roman state, whose course will on
> The way it takes, cracking ten thousand curbs
> Of more strong link asunder than can ever
> Appear in your impediment.
>
> (I.i.66–71)

In the face of this image of undeviating, unstoppable
motion, the citizens' own attempts at 'proceeding' seem
puny and hesitant indeed. Menenius may well be invoking
the prophetic vision of an imperial destiny of which he
himself cannot be conscious.[6] But the syntax through which
his own words move is no less important than the image.

The power of this massive motion can be measured by the ten thousand curbs which the Roman state will leave devastated in its wake, as signs of its own invincible progress. Menenius's sentence enacts this relentless movement by the links or curbs across which it propels itself, gathering power as it leaves them behind—'as . . . as . . . whose . . . cracking . . . more . . . than . . .'.

Menenius employs two particular tactics typical of the language of power in the play as a whole. One is the use of a relative clause that propels the scene forward, as if by virtue of a second or afterthought that occurs as the sentence itself is in motion. The other is a comparative construction of crushing elaboration, which deprecates the possibility of comparison even as it makes it.[7] Cominius will provide a memorable example when he heralds Martius's approach on the battlefield:

The shepherd knows not thunder from a tabor,
More than I know the sound of Martius' tongue
From every meaner man.

(I.vi.25–7)

Cominius's genuine joy does not obscure the derision intrinsic to this figure. Martius will eventually hear the laughter of the gods at the humiliating difference between Olympus and a molehill.

The First Citizen was ready with several explanations of Martius's motives: safety in numbers. Menenius has more than one ploy for putting the plebeians in their place. The most memorable of these is his 'pretty tale' of the belly and its mutinous members. This steadies and generalises the opening scene's concerns with hunger and anger and language, the ways in which words moderate or exacerbate the violences of physical need, and the violence to which it gives rise. How far does Menenius convince his immediate auditors onstage? How far do we suppose that he convinced a theatre audience in 1608 or a reader in 1623? How far do we suppose that he was supposed to?

Shakespeare and his contemporaries lived with the permanent threat of dearth, the memory and fear of hunger as a widespread human and social fact. The social historians Walter and Wrightson provide some helpful perspectives on Menenius's fable.

> It is difficult to exaggerate the extent to which people in the late sixteenth and early seventeenth century were conscious of the threat of dearth. Periodic harvest disaster and food shortage were the spectre which haunted early modern Europe, one of the principal factors contributing to the profound insecurity of the age.[8]

Walter and Wrightson advance evidence for a deep-seated reluctance to resort to force both on the part of the victims of dearth and on the part of civil authorities faced with its social consequences. They argue that the very permanence and magnitude of the threat posed by dearth created the need for a corresponding weight of explanation to control it. This complex body of explanation was compounded of various elements:

> ways of accounting for dearth which, having their origins in the experiences of different sections of society, blended together into a coherent explanation which was potentially satisfactory to all and informed both administrative and popular responses to such crises.[9]

They conclude, 'What is significant is less that dearth in England provoked occasional outbreaks of disorder than that it led to so few'.[10]

Menenius does not concert all the specific explanations described by Walter and Wrightson, but there is a correspondence to be found in the form and method of his tactics. In fact he does refer in passing to the most familiar of explanations that 'For the dearth,/The gods, not the patricians, make it' (I.i.71–2). This makes a nominal gesture towards the 'doctrine of judgements', the idea that the three great judgements (dearth, plague and the sword) were punishment for sin, a doctrine so familiar to Shakespeare's audience that it requires no more than a nod to activate it. How far Menenius's listeners are convinced by it is another matter.

But the main weight of his explanations is thrown into the parable of the belly. Shakespeare's audience would be familiar from a variety of sources with the image of the body politic. Indeed the overfamiliarity of the fable's components is precisely what makes its interpretation difficult. It is a question of how seriously Menenius offers his interpretation to the plebeians and to us, and how seriously they and we take it. There are many more ways of playing this scene than Reuben Brower acknowledges when he makes the following confident interpretation of its tone:

> The good-natured insolence and sturdy candor, the tough repartee of the exchanges, belong to a game played between patrician and people. The 'Belly-smile' of the patrician, and the 'great toe' of the plebeian, both help to impart the feeling of healthy relatedness in a civil society.[11]

Such a good-natured attitude surely ought to wither in the face of Menenius's forthcoming reference to his auditors as 'rats'. Nevertheless, it is impossible to dispel the sense that this is indeed a kind of 'game' played not only between patrician and people, but also between playwright and audience.

If Menenius's fable is taken seriously it is difficult not to notice its fallacies. The patrician belly is actually supposed to be *worse off* than the plebeian members ('that all/From me do back receive the flour of all, / And leave me but the bran')? This defies belief as a general statement of the relative diet of the patricians and the people, but it doubly defies belief that this is what is happening in the present dearth. Fabling apart, what *has* happened to the distribution of food in Rome here and now? Are 'the store-houses crammed with grain', as the First Citizen claimed, or are they not?

In any case the polity of the body which Menenius proposes is in its own terms rather suspicious, as M. J. B. Allen notes:

> Every thinking member of Shakespeare's audience would have been struck by the fact that Menenius' version, though speciously persuasive and internally consistent, was nevertheless the incorrect, the heretical, the dangerously heretical version. For any allegory that elevated the stomach over the heart or head was obviously portraying a topsy-turvy, chaotic vision of things where the great chain of correspondences had been swept aside by the wolf of appetite.[12]

This seems convincing, but even a thinking member can suffer a moment of weakness, and it is still possible for a thinking member of a modern audience to be swayed by Menenius and his fable. Bradley thought Menenius 'a pleasant and wise old gentleman', whom the play regarded with 'unmingled approval'.[13] And Kitto is not alone in attributing to the idea of the body politic a transcendent reality informing the play as a whole.

> Even the uninstructed reader of Shakespeare apprehends easily enough that to Shakespeare, and presumably to his audiences also, the idea of a divinely appointed Order is basic: that 'the body politic' was not a tired metaphor, that 'the deputy elected by the Lord' was at least a poetic reality. For reassurance the layman can turn to the experts, to Professor L. C. Knights's British Academy Lecture for instance, and learn that it is indeed true; that

in Shakespeare there is a living connexion between
concepts like Order, Nature, Providence, the peaceful
State, the anointed King, Goodness, Fruitfulness, Love.[14]

It would be easy to scoff at Kitto's gullibility. There are other
experts who will tell us that a tired metaphor was exactly
what 'the body politic' was by 1607–8, indeed that it was so
tired as to be actually dead. 'The Death of a Political
Metaphor' is the title of one relevant essay.[15] But Kitto's
innocence is a useful reminder that the question of belief,
political or otherwise, is not something which can be
decisively regulated by an intellectual élite or thinking
members of professional Shakespearian experts. We may
take it that neither in Shakespeare's time nor our own is it
only the supposedly unthinking members of the audience
who are disposed to trust Menenius.

In fact, Menenius's fable is not quite as easy to see
through as Allen suggests. After all, it is not absolutely clear
that Menenius's 'dangerously heretical' model of the body
does elevate the stomach over the heart or head. It is true that
the head and heart play no role at all in the first part of his
speech, but one might understand this to be a purely tactical
and even tactful omission: this squalid quarrel between the
belly and the body's members is obviously beneath them.
The Citizen introduces them when he refers, albeit
ironically, to 'the kingly crown'd head' and the 'counsellor
heart', and this could be understood as an implicit
restatement of a more orthodox polity of the body and a
rebuke to Menenius's heretical version. But it is not
necessary to see the two models in opposition to each other.
In the version preserved in Camden's *Remaines*, the
mutinous members only seek the advice of the heart after
they have begun to feel the effect of three days' starvation.[16]
And Menenius *does* in due course make reference to 'the
heart', if not exactly to 'the head', in his description of the
belly's redistribution of food 'through the rivers of your
blood/Even to the court, the heart, to th'seat o'th'brain (I.i.

134–5). This is a splendidly mysterious place, evidently the residence of the body's highest authority, whether this is called the heart or the brain. Brockbank notes, 'The mysterious relationship between brain and heart often perplexes Shakespeare's language'.[17] And the mysterious relationship of this mumbo-jumbo to any actual political reality would certainly perplex Menenius's hearers, both on stage and in the audience, if they are thinking enough to ask such awkward questions. Where exactly in republican Rome can you find 'the Court'—in the Senate? But Menenius is going to identify the senators with the belly. Martius believes in what he calls 'the heart of generosity' (I.i. 210), but where does this figure find a material, political reality? And who exactly in the constitution of Jacobean England, however it is described, would correspond to Menenius's selflessly executive belly? These are the questions to which Menenius's mystifications give rise even as they are supposed to mask them.

It is impossible to be certain what effect Menenius's fable has on the plebeians. His closing words suggest that he knows that he has made little real impression on them, though a little later he will say that they are 'almost thoroughly persuaded'. Does he intend them to hear and understand that he is now calling those same people 'rats' whom he began by addressing as 'mine honest neighbours'? If the 'rats' feel a surge of renewed vigour at the prospect of violent strife, they are instantly confronted by a new antagonist, who wears no masks and scorns verbal calculation.

No major Shakespearian character is as instantly voluble as Caius Martius. In the theatre it is difficult to attend to what he is saying, because we are given so little chance to size the actor up before he launches into torrential speech. The eye has a chance to dwell on Hamlet and Othello and Macbeth on their first appearances; other people do most of the talking. Nobody makes an audience flinch as instantly and instinctively as Martius does. Martius asks the plebeians a question ('What's the matter . . .?'), but he does not get an answer to it. This is not surprising. The way he uses words does not show much interest in the possibility of dialogue.

When we look at the shape of his speech on the page we can see that it possesses exactly that quality of 'resolution' which the citizens were in search of. That is to say, a kind of 'certainty' that depends on the manipulation of sharp antitheses, of absolute oppositions and self-destroying comparisons. Just as the citizens tried to characterise their sense of themselves by characterising Martius as their 'chief enemy', so Martius—but with how much greater confidence and precision—confirms and expresses his sense of himself by characterising *them*. There is something terrifying but also exhilarating in the very impact of such certainty, something that cuts athwart whatever feelings we may have about the *content* of what he is saying. The content itself is simple enough: the absolute unreliability of the people whom he is addressing. Yet the very zest with which his speech engages with the objects of its contempt ensures that his speech is not itself predictable.[18] Though he says one and the same thing over and over again, we are continually surprised by the ways in which he says it: 'you are no surer, no,/Than . . .'—than what?—'Than is the coal of fire upon the ice,/Or hailstone in the sun' (I.i. 171–3). Fire and ice: the conjunction of these extremes serves to characterise Martius himself as much as the people to whom he refers. The images of fire and water and melting so casually invoked here will return in the latter stages of the play with increasingly explicit significance.

There is a derisive wit at work throughout his summoning of contraries: lions and hares, foxes and geese, fire and ice. It is a wit that sounds as if it were drawing on proverbial wisdom,[19] like the image of the ludicrous creature who tries to swim with 'fins of lead' (I.i. 178–9). Might not his auditors find some humour, however ruefully, in this sort of violent banter?[20] Is Martius entirely in earnest, or is he—as the tribunes will later say of Menenius—known well enough? There is a lot of comedy in the play that depends on characters taking themselves more seriously than we do. But around Martius himself, the nervous, flickering comedy has something to do with our knowing how dangerous it would be to fail to take him at his word.

The news of imminent war is as welcome to Martius as the news of the granting of tribunes should be to the people. The 'business' of the plebeians has been, for Martius, a risible distraction from the real business of the city. Now he is back in the limelight. This is the way the tribunes think of him, but it is sharply at odds with the impression we have ourselves received. Left alone on stage, they start working out the implications of Martius's accepting the post of second-in-command with all the avidity of born political commentators, mongering their political projections, speculating about the percentage points that Martius is likely to gain by accepting a place below the first. Yet the uncalculating ease with which Martius accepts his commission makes us feel that he takes little interest in the kind of fame about which they are so bustlingly curious. So far from there being any friction between Cominius and Martius and Titus Lartius, the divided command in fact serves to show how thoroughly amiable are the working relations between the three men.

In Plutarch, Aufidius is not mentioned until Martius decides to desert to the Volsces. Shakespeare introduces him into the play early on to establish and sustain the idea of what North calls the 'marvelous private hate' between them.[21] And perhaps something more and other than hate. Aufidius confirms and enlarges our impression that Rome has real business in the outside world. The Romans and Volscians are customary, even natural antagonists, and the wars between them are a regular business. No particular motive is required to justify this war: here the contrast with the English history plays is marked. It is just what men and states naturally do, to battle for survival. Aufidius helps to naturalise this view of men's business when he says that "Tis sworn' between Martius and himself (I.ii. 35). We do not pause to wonder how literally he means this; it simply confirms that he relishes the prospect of doing business with Rome's star performer as much as we know Martius does with him—like two prize-fighters whose reputations so far precede them that they have no need of any personal knowledge to feel an intimate bond.

The contrasts with which we have been impressed are becoming clearer—the contrasts between two kinds of opposition or confrontation: the enmity between Martius and the masses, the enmity between Martius and Aufidius: and related to these personalised enmities, the different aspects of the city, its internal and external antagonisms.

The next scene, however, sketches for the first time in the play quite different images of relationship. It is dominated by women. It is the only scene in the first half of the play that obviously takes place indoors or inside. (Act 3 Scene 2 is probably set in Martius's house, but this fact is not stressed). In this respect it will be balanced by the scene in the second half in which Martius is received by Aufidius in his house. It also looks forward to the two other occasions on which we will see this trio of women together, Volumnia, Virgilia and Valeria. On both occasions they will greet Martius on his triumphal returns to Rome, first as the conqueror of Corioles, and then as he stands poised to become the conqueror of Rome itself. At these great public moments they will represent the concerted claims of the family life which the women uphold in their men's absence.

Shakespeare got some clues for Martius's mother from North's Plutarch, but he turned them to astonishing effect. Plutarch says that Martius 'being left an orphan by his father, was brought up under his mother a widowe'.[22] It is not explicitly stated that this lack of a father was responsible for his 'lacke of education',[23] but Shakespeare's imagination went vigorously to work on the mother's part in bringing up Martius and on her responsibility for his 'education', or the

lack of it. He got another clue to the grip of their
relationship in Plutarch's account of the source and goal of
Martius's valour in battle: 'the only thing that made him to
love honour, was the joye he sawe his mother dyd take of
him'.[24] Apart from these hints this mother plays no part in
Plutarch's narrative until her son is ready to conquer Rome
and she is persuaded to make a last appeal to him.
Shakespeare entirely excises the religious aura surrounding
this appeal, the vision which moves Valeria to suggest the
women's deputation to Martius, and the subsequently
pious thanksgiving in which the women get a temple and an
image of Fortune built to thank them for their trouble.
Shakespeare makes the characters in his play frequently
appeal to the gods, but he is more interested in the awe that
they feel towards and inspire in each other—interested, that
is, in human *godding*, to adapt Martius's own extraordinary
coinage (V.iii. 11). He makes Martius's mother the prime
author of these visions of divinity that accumulate around
the figure of her son.

So far we have seen and imagined Martius face to face
with others. It seems his natural attitude: he is happy to live
by the preposition 'against'. Now for the first time we see the
women at his back, his mother and his wife. They are
different kinds of women, and they stand in different
relations to him. But they are both the women from whom
he sets out to work, and the women who await his return. In
the course of the play, we shall see him return to them twice
and depart from them twice.

It is the question of his leaving and returning that
dominates their thoughts. There are soft-conscienced
readers who shrink with horror from Volumnia's pride and
joy in her son. But how easily does this pride and joy come
to her? The difficulty in organising our thoughts and feelings
about her centres on this doubt. From her first speech, she
makes it clear that she knows that she has renounced
something:

When yet he was but tender-bodied, and the only son of my womb; when youth with comeliness plucked all gaze his way; when for a day of kings' entreaties, a mother should not sell him an hour from her beholding; I, considering how honour would become such a person—that it was no better than picture-like to hang by th'wall, if renown made it not stir—was pleased to let him seek danger where he was like to find fame. To a cruel war I sent him . . . .

(I.iii. 5–14)

She has cast him out or sent him forth before his time. Picking up a clue from the image she uses of Hecuba's 'breasts', we might say that she has ripped him untimely, not from his mother's womb but from his mother's breast. Like Lady Macbeth she is made to use an image which overtly disparages the mother's nurturing power.[25] Later on we may hear a strangely inverted echo of the woman behind Macbeth, when the woman behind Martius rebukes him with the words, 'You might have been enough the man you are,/With striving less to be so' (III.ii. 19–20). Lady Macbeth had to screw up her husband to the sticking place of his manhood:

When you durst do it, then you were a man;
And to be more than what you were, you would
Be so much more the man.

(Macbeth, I.vii. 49–51)

But Volumnia's son has long since reached a sticking place, and her task will be to try to unscrew him from it. Is there any milk left in Martius? Menenius will mutter in despair that there is 'no more mercy in him than there is milk in a male tiger' (V.iv. 28–9). Volumnia is at the source of the many images projected onto her son, of a being entirely composed of 'blood'—a 'thing of blood', as Cominius will call him (II.ii. 109).

Volumnia's role is not just one in which nature has cast her. This scene invites us to observe the means by which she has made it her own, and to wonder at the pains and pleasures it has brought her. Take her response to Virgilia's inquiry as to what she would do if Martius were killed: 'Then his good report should have been my son' (I.iii. 20). It is easy to read this as callousness, rolling glibly off the tongue. But to read it as such would itself be glib, before entertaining the thought that women whose men run the constant risk of death may do well to forefeel their bereavement. Nor would one easily say to such a woman's face that she had no right to her pride in that good report. There might be a momentary pause before she gives this answer. But even if she answers without hesitation, we could not conclude that she has never felt any pain in knowing that this would always be her answer to such a question.

One open element in our sense of this scene is the extent to which Volumnia's words are directed at Virgilia. This is partly a question of the tension between the two women. Whose house is this? Plutarch tells us that after his marriage Martius continued to live in his mother's house, but in performance there is no means of being sure to whom this space belongs. Volumnia initiates and dominates the speech, but it is Virgilia who quietly asserts her authority over the space. One can read into Volumnia's merciless recitation of the ethos by which *she* has lived a hostility to the woman whose pacific temperament constitutes an implicit critique of her whole way of life. Virgilia's stubborn refusal to play the part which Volumnia imagines for her— singing, and expressing herself 'in a more comfortable sort' (I.iii. 1–2)—constitutes an implied rebuke to Volumnia's triumph over fear. One might even entertain a mischievous possibility that would run sharply counter to the traditional idealisation of Virgilia, by supposing that she deliberately *exaggerates* her real fearfulness in order to tease her mother-in-law ('O Jupiter, no blood!'—knowing that this is *exactly* what will most irritate Volumnia). They fight over Virgilia's solemness, they fight over the little boy, they fight over going out to visit their neighbours: it might as well be Ibsen.

But one could also read a kind of goodwill into Volumnia's attitude to Virgilia—a desire that for her *own* sake the younger woman should conquer her fear as she herself has done.[26] Virgilia's agony of apprehension is precisely the state from which Volumnia has freed herself by an act of pure will. Has she succeeded in freeing herself entirely? Volumnia's words may be directed at herself rather than (or as well as) at Virgilia. The image of Volumnia fluctuates between two extremes, the abruptly self-righteous guardian of an ethos, and the rapt, ecstatic visionary. Through the repetitions of her litany, she confirms her countenance against the memory of her child's tender body. The syntax of the sentence that begins, 'When yet he was but tender-bodied . . .', requires both from Volumnia and the actress playing her a breathtaking stamina such as only long training can produce.

And Virgilia? Valeria mockingly compares her to Penelope, the model of the patient wife awaiting the return of her wandering warrior husband, a single man in the vast world. Volumnia had invoked, albeit invidiously, another mighty image of womanhood in the figure of Hecuba. Virgilia resists the likenesses and roles which are thrust at her by the other women, confining herself to the simplest of statements: 'No, at a word'. She rejects the invitation to 'go visit the good lady that lies in'; she will 'not over the threshold' till her lord returns from the wars. Virgilia gently but firmly disparages a women's collective domain centering on the processes of childbirth in which men have no necessary role. She forgoes the pleasure of the women's 'mirth' that we glimpse in Valeria's sociable chatter, in favour of an anxious, tenacious loyalty to the memory of her husband and the promise of his return. Yet this scene does plant in our minds the image of concerted female suffering and action such as will re-emerge to massive effect at the climax of the play. The third and last occasion on

which we see these women together is in the great
supplication scene (V.iii.). There we will feel the force of
Virgilia's crossing a threshold to align herself with the other
women and with the claims of childbirth.

The juxtaposition of scenes throws Virgilia's renun-
ciation of 'mirth' into quietly pathetic relief when we see
how much mirth her husband finds in his work and can
share with his colleagues. The echoes of her 'solemness'
overlap with the buoyant pleasure that her husband takes in
the little exchange with Titus Lartius before they get down
to business (I.iv. 1–7). This man is happy at his work;
perhaps *only* happy when he is at work.

The mirth is strictly temporary. 'Enter Martius, cursing'
(I.iv. 30): this was the attitude in which he made his first
appearance in the play, and now it is repeated. It is one of the
several 'postures' in which we will remember him. 'You
shames of Rome!' There is something in the very smell of
other people's fear that inspires him to exult in his own
fearlessness. In the market-place his revulsion from the
smell of the common people may seem merely like a
personal fastidiousness. But in the teeth of death he smells
something more than skin-deep in their shrinking, and it is
the smell of physical corruption that in return he wishes on
them. This note of visceral loathing will return at a climactic
moment, when he speaks of 'the reek o'th'rotten fens'
(III.iii. 121). 'Reek' and 'rotten' recur elsewhere: Cominius
will turn Martius into a figure for the god of war himself,
when he imagines him, unforgettably, 'Run reeking o'er the
lives of men, as if/'Twere a perpetual spoil' (II.ii. 119–20).

By then the legend has taken root. What exactly happens
at the siege of Corioles, when Martius performs his reckless,
heroic feat? We know what people later suppose to have
happened, in the official myth that envelopes him, that he
captured the city single-handed. But to do this *literally* he
would indeed have to be a superman or a demi-god. In
Plutarch, Martius follows the fleeing Volsces into the city
'with very fewe men to helpe him', and 'with a wonderfull

courage and valliantness' makes a 'lane' through the midst
of the enemy, which gives Lartius time to bring up the rest of
the troops.[27] There is no mention of the gates being shut
behind him. Shakespeare could have chosen to represent all
this in narrative, but instead he chose the more difficult
option of showing—or half-showing—what Martius did.
He makes Martius enter the city entirely alone, just as later
he makes him leave the city of Rome entirely alone,
unaccompanied by the friends that Plutarch gives him. This
creates the opportunity for Lartius's obituary notice, but it
also creates a massive problem in the nature of Martius's re-
entrance. The Folio's stage-direction here reads, 'Enter
Martius bleeding, assaulted by the Enemy'. How do the
gates open? Do we suppose that Martius opened them
himself, or that they somehow give way, being pinned still
only with 'rushes', as the Volscian senator had said?
Obviously the effect on stage is that it is astounding to find
that he is still alive, fighting for his life, against impossible
odds.

William Empson seizes on the problem with a wonderful
glee in the course of examining the resources of the Globe
theatre.[28] He uses Lartius's call for the siege-ladders to
construct an ingenious scenario that has Martius fighting his
way backwards up the stairs inside the gates, to re-emerge on
the upper-stage that represents the city walls. His
reappearance would enable the others to get the siege-
ladders up and it would, Empson argues, more plausibly
support the illusion that Martius has somehow captured the
city single-handed than the horribly awkward business with
the gates. Empson explains this latter as a second-best
option provided for a touring version of the play in theatres
that lacked the Globe's balcony. So that what we have is a
conflated text of the two different versions, one of them
distinctly more plausible.

This is not much ado about nothing, though it may not be
quite as important as Empson thinks. However it is done,
the important effect must be that Martius makes an inroad

into the city, which against all the odds he succeeds in holding long enough for the others to turn it to maximum advantage. Of course he does not literally capture the city single-handed, but he does 'alone' make all the difference. What is useful about Empson's theory is that it helps him to stress the gap between what an audience sees for itself and what the characters subsequently make of the events.

> What the play keeps on saying is that he must be a demi-god, because no human being could capture a walled city single-handed. We do not know whether he believes it himself, because his rule of politeness keeps him silent, but he appears to accept it when he destroys himself by telling the Volscians, 'Alone I did it', in Corioli. But we of the Globe audience saw what really happened, so we know that it wasn't superhuman after all, though of course splendidly brave, vigorous, and resourceful, like a coup by Biggles. It is rather shocking that such a good first Act could become forgotten.[29]

This scepticism is invaluably bracing. Too much exposure to dutiful expositions of the play's imagery and what it tells us about the central figure can dull the reader's interest in exactly how and why and by whom and to what effect these images are *produced*. A theatre audience is naturally inclined to be at once more involved and more sceptical in exercising its feelings and wits on the palpable difference between what the characters on stage do and what they say. The members of a theatre audience can recall what they saw for themselves (whatever the details of the staging), when they listen to the grandiloquent terms that Cominius finds to describe these events in his formal oration to the Senate. They may wonder exactly what his figure of speech means, when he says that Martius entered

> The mortal gate of th'city, which he painted
> With shunless destiny.

> (II.ii. 111–12)

They may remember the bleeding assaulted figure whom Lartius felt the need to 'fetch off', when they hear Cominius go on to say that Martius

> aidless came off,
> And with a sudden reinforcement struck
> Corioles like a planet.
>
> (II.ii. 112–14)

They may even remember that Cominius did not see all this for himself.

Empson exaggerates the extent to which Martius's feat at Corioles transforms the way people think of him, when he says that Shakespeare was 'very specific about Coriolanus, making him a man to whom the tragic story would be unlikely to happen, were it not for this initial event'.[30] On the contrary, both before and after 'this initial event' we are given clear indications that Martius was *bound* to do something extraordinary sooner or later. In the speech that seals the legend, Cominius tells us that after his startling debut against Tarquin, Martius 'lurch'd all swords of the garland' in no less than seventeen subsequent battles (II.ii. 100–1). It cannot come as a complete surprise that—to use the sporting metaphors that Martius nowadays seems bound to provoke in readers, including Empson—such a consistently high scorer should at some point break a world record. Empson underplays Martius's sheer readiness for conversion into legend, but he does focus very acutely on the decisiveness of what happens at Corioles for Martius's subsequent career, and above all, on the gap that separates his actions from the subsequent myth: 'the buildings of fancy', to adapt a phrase of his mother's.

Martius will turn into a legend, but the legend is not built on thin air. This is why it is essential for an audience to be physically impressed by the actor playing Martius, to feel his impact, so that we can understand how the other characters come to think of him as superhuman, and how he may come to think this himself. It is not just a matter of physical strength, but of mind over matter, or 'spirit' over the body.[31] Cominius says that 'his doubled spirit/ Requicken'd what in flesh was fatigate' (II.ii. 116–17): the Latinism of 'fatigate' itself distances the weariness of the flesh. When he chooses the soldiers to take against the Antiates' men of trust, Martius says that the ones he wants are simply those 'that are most willing' (I.vi. 67) and 'so minded' (I.vi. 73). That there is nothing in truth superhuman about him is proved by the exhaustion that understandably comes over him after the battle, and he confesses that his 'memory is tired'.

Conquering a city virtually single-handed might be enough for most heroes, but what Martius is really interested in is having a round with Aufidius, face to face. He is ready for him now that his own face is covered in blood, now that he looks 'as he were flay'd' (I.vi. 22). That's Martius all right, says Cominius, as this terrifying apparition approaches: 'He has the stamp of Martius' (I.vi. 23). A stamp guarantees authenticity, and this is the appearance in which Martius feels at home. We may remember this later, when the blood has had time to dry and his body has settled into an object that can be inspected by others, when he is no longer an apparition to inspire terror and wonder, but an object to be read and judged and approved.   ·

The speech which Martius addresses to Cominius's troops is staggeringly different from the one he addressed to the 'shames of Rome' who were beaten to their trenches a little earlier. Where Martius had rounded on his men with withering scorn, Cominius has treated his with respect and maintained their morale ('Breathe you, my friends; well fought'). There is no means of knowing whether the soldiers who were 'beat back to their trenches' at Corioles behaved worse than the soldiers whom Cominius rallies 'as it were in retire'. It is true that Martius's example does in the end have some effect on his soldiers, in that they follow him (and

Lartius) back into Corioles. But it is not obvious that Martius's way of treating them gets better results than Cominius's, and one of the reasons that Martius can now address such a rousingly patriotic speech to these men is that he can appeal to a sense of fellowship which Cominius's comradely treatment of them has kept alive. After Martius's heroic speech, it is Cominius who more quietly and pragmatically bolsters their resolution by addressing them as 'my fellows', and promising that they shall 'Divide in all with us' (I.vi. 85–7).

'Oh me alone, make you a sword of me'—the Folio text makes Martius himself shout this line, as he is taken up in the soldiers' arms. The punctuation and hence intonation of the line are disputed: is it a question or an exclamation? Some editors suppose the words to be shouted not by Martius but by the soldiers in response to Martius's call to arms. Brockbank gives it to *All* in his Arden edition: 'O me alone! Make you a sword of me!' (I.vi. 76). It is a reasonable supposition, but one may weigh the significance that such a doubt should occur at all. The fact is that this is the one moment in the play at which Martius *is* at one with the many, his voice rousing and blending with theirs. For the first and last time in the play, we see and hear him at the head of a mass of people, literally taken up in their arms. Whether he speaks the line himself or whether the soldiers speak it together, he has achieved a pinnacle of desire. He is the sword of his people. His words are transformed into the gesture of pure intent, in which he and a great mass of people are at one. He has concluded his rallying speech by referring to himself in the third person for the first time in the play, as he and they all together do as he says:

Wave thus to express his disposition,
And follow Martius.

(I.vi. 74–5)[32]

After this the scene in which he comes face to face with

Aufidius is bound to come as an anti-climax. The taunts and vaunts that they throw at each other must strike us as perfunctory (I.viii. 1–13). Wrenching up their power to the highest is what they really want to do, and they can do that best without words. The loyalty of the 'condemned seconds' who come to Aufidius's aid stands in ironic contrast to the 'seconds' who failed to materialise when Martius careered into Corioles. This sort of combat is different, and the enmity between the two men can only be settled by death. In fact the anti-climax of this scene has been subtly prepared for by the tiny glimpse of Titus Lartius that precedes the renewal of the field-battle (I.vii.). It prepares us for the knowledge that war has a massive aftermath in which gains have to be held on to, losses explained, rewards and punishments dispensed. Martius has escaped with alacrity from the administration—it is hardly his forte. But soon he will be faced with a more protracted and painful aftermath. He will have to live with his new-found name and fame: they are public property. And eventually he will have to count the cost of the shame he inflicts on others, a shame that will especially fester in the enemy he loves to hate, Aufidius.

· 2 ·

'Acclamations hyperbolical'

The opening scenes have shown us some of the ways in which other people think about Martius—the plebeians, the patricians, Aufidius, the women. These are the four primary views of him that the first Act establishes, weaving a series of contrasts and connections. These all attempt to fix Martius, or get a fix on him, and as the play progresses we will become increasingly conscious of this need to transform him into various kinds of image—a monument, a machine, a monster, a god, a thing.

It is from his friend and colleague Titus Lartius that we get the first real hint of what is to come. Up until now nobody has thought of him as a superman, least of all the common soldiers. When they watch him rush madly and heroically into the city all on his own, they assume that he is done for: 'To th'pot, I warrant him'. Titus Lartius also assumes that he is done for, but the impromptu obituary which he composes strikes a note distinctly more elevated than the soldiers' collective shrug—almost comically so:

> Oh noble fellow!
> Who sensibly outdares his senseless sword,
> And when it bows, stand'st up. Thou art left,
>   Martius:
> A carbuncle entire, as big as thou art,

23

Were not so rich a jewel. Thou wast a soldier
Even to Cato's wish, not fierce and terrible
Only in strokes, but with thy grim looks and
The thunder-like percussion of thy sounds
Thou mad'st thine enemies shake, as if the world
Were feverous and did tremble.

                                              (I.iv. 52–61)

The other patricians will often be found imputing to
Martius an inhuman constancy. Here we encounter the
image of a flesh-and-blood so rigid that it shames the
inanimate sword into the 'sensibility' that it has scornfully
vacated. It is partly the timing of the speech that gives it a
comical tilt. There is a lot of bad timing in the play: many
things get said too early and too late. This epitaph is
distinctly premature. Martius is the kind of man about
whom it would be easier to speak in the past tense, as Lartius
does here, and as Cominius does in his more studied oration
before the Senate back in Rome. There might almost be a
hint of apology in the soldiers' nudging Lartius into the
realisation that Martius is not dead yet. 'Oh', Lartius gasps.
  If coolly inspected, Lartius's speech teeters on the edge of
absurdity. But it focuses an important problem about the
status of speech in the play, and the ways in which readers
and audiences react to it and judge it. Lartius is speaking in
the heat and excitement of distress, and in performance an
audience will lend a more sympathetic ear to his hyperbole
than a reader. Nor will the shrewdest ear find risibility
throughout the entire speech, for its second half is
noticeably more controlled. The appeal to Cato's[1] authority
steadies Lartius's language into a weightier idiom until it
reaches its controlled climax—'as if the world/Were
feverous and did tremble'. He has turned from the queasy
images of Martius's intrinsic qualities to the more palpable
effects which Martius has on others.
  This is the prelude to the legend of 'Coriolanus': it is
progressively established by a carefully paced sequence of

three scenes. First there is the naming that takes place on the battlefield (I.ix.); then there is the triumphal entry into Rome (II.i); and finally Cominius's formal oration before the Senate (II.ii.).

Martius does not enjoy the aftermath of war: it taxes his patience. When he tries to forestall the burden of praise, Cominius rebukes him with a telling speech:

> You shall not be
> The grave of your deserving; Rome must know
> The value of her own.
>
> (I.ix. 19–21)

There is a concealed doubleness to this 'must'. Rome both needs to know the value of her own, but she also has a right to it. The value of her own what? The absence of a noun contributes to the sense of reflexiveness, the thought of Rome knowing *herself*, of thinking herself for the city she is (to adapt one of Martius's own later pregnant expressions). Is Martius the means by which Rome can know herself, or is he exactly what throws this possibility into confusion? T. S. Eliot has a deceptively throwaway line in the 'Triumphal March' of his 'Coriolan': 'We hardly knew ourselves that day, or knew the City'.[2]

How can Rome know the value of Martius? What Rome owes to him can only be known if his deeds are translated into words. Only words can preserve the memory of deeds. But it is this passage of deeds into words that rouses Martius's deepest suspicions and fears. No words can 'express' his 'disposition' more surely than a gesture, a physical action such as wielding his sword. What words then could express his 'value'? What *is* his value? His value is his 'valour', but no words can begin to express the value of valour.

Norman Rabkin observes that there is a philosophical argument behind the disagreement between the two men (or extractable from it).[3] Cominius's position is that the idea of

honour will wither if someone does not 'stand' for it;
Martius's position is that the idea of honour will be
corrupted if anyone does. For himself, he wants to believe
that his actions live entirely in the present, that as Cominius
later says, he can 'spend the time to end it' (II.ii. 128). Or as
Rabkin paraphrases it, for Martius 'honor is a quality of
action, not of action's effects'.[4] Martius wants to believe that
the value of his actions is proof against time, not because he
has any hope of deserving to transcend actuality, but
because by perpetual repetition he may escape shaming the
impossibly lofty ideal of honour which he serves. He would
laugh with scornful incredulity at Hotspur's boyish self-
confidence:

> By heaven, methinks it were an easy leap
> To pluck bright honour from the pale-face'd moon;
> Or dive into the bottom of the deep,
> . . .
> And pluck up drowned honour by the locks;. . .
> (*Henry IV, Part I*, I.iii. 201–5)

Martius is not given to such charmingly reckless fantasy.
When he thinks of the moon it marks an unreachable
distance—the plebeians throwing their caps (I.i. 211–12),
Valeria's chastity (V.iii. 65). Honour for him is not
something you can pluck down or pluck up, like Hotspur's
superman. His is a peculiarly austere form of idealism,
tenaciously self-punishing and bitterly punitive towards
anyone who fails to honour his own right to it and Rome's
need for it. This is the value that Rome needs to know, not
the value of her *own*.

These are considerations which the play itself is only just
beginning to excite. Martius has so far given little expression
to what he positively believes in. He has talked about
bravery and patriotism, but so far these virtues have simply
been proved in action. Now, in this pivotal scene (I.ix.),
these and other virtues must begin to suffer explanation, of

their sources and goals, their motives and consequences.

Martius rejects with contempt the material goods with which Cominius tries to reward him, but he rejects with anger the instinctive clamour with which the soldiers greet their approval of this gesture. He had not meant it to be a gesture:[5]

> May these same instruments, which you profane,
> Never sound more! When drums and trumpets shall
> I'th'field prove flatterers, let courts and cities be
> Made all of false-fac'd soothing! When steel grows
> Soft as the parasite's silk, let him be made
> An ovator for th'wars!
>
> (I.ix. 41–6)

Why does this touch him on the raw? We can tell that it does so by the extremism of the imagery (steel and silk) and the confusion of the syntax (what does the 'him' refer to?). His auditors are no more likely to understand exactly what that last sentence means than the editors who struggle to make sense of the Folio's 'Ouerture' ('ovator'? 'coverture'? 'armature'?).[6] His sudden rage may be something to do with the sheer effect that the sound has on him. He is at home with the sound of drums and trumpets because what they signify is the call to action, in which he will come face to face with the enemy.[7] These are the sounds which he associates with looking outwards and forwards, towards the enemy; they make his blood rush. Now all of a sudden these sounds mark a moment at which everyone is looking at him, at which he is the centre of attention.

In the midst of the battle Cominius quickly yielded to Martius's will, but in its aftermath he reasserts his authority. Is there embarrassment in the facetious lines in which he says that they will have to put Martius in manacles before reasoning with him (I.ix. 54–7)? But Martius is being embarrassing. He is refusing to play the game, to accept the gratitude that his people wish to express, and which, as

Cominius insists, he has an *obligation* to accept. But a name
is difficult to refuse because it is only a word. A name is
something which other people give you, which helps them
to recognise you. And recognition—knowing the value of
her own—is what Rome insists on exacting from Martius.
From now on he will bear 'th'addition' of 'Coriolanus'.[8]

One must make the point that it is a problem for readers
and critics to know how to refer to this man and that this
repeats a problem that is one of the play's subjects. Most
people who write about the play decide to refer to him as
'Coriolanus' (without the inverted commas), thus
imperceptibly fortifying the grip that the man and the name
have on each other. I shall continue to refer to him as
'Martius' with a view to preserving the sense of imposition
and strangeness in the name 'Coriolanus'. The word
'Martius' is heard almost exactly twice as many times in the
play as the word 'Coriolanus'.[9]

There remains in this scene the odd and unexpected detail
of Martius's appeal for the release of a poor Volscian whose
name he has forgotten. This is a good instance of
Shakespeare's interest in purposively embarrassing the
smooth running of ceremony. In Plutarch the Volscian is
'an olde friende and hoste of mine, an honest wealthie man'.
There is no suggestion that Martius suddenly glimpsed him
in the recent battle, and there is no question of his forgetting
the man's name. But ho less important than these details is
the timing of Martius's request for the man's release. In
Plutarch it goes graciously with Martius's response to
Cominius's efforts to reward him in public, a response in
which he accepts 'a goodly horse with a capparison' but
refuses the first choice and tenth share of the spoils. His
request for the Volscian's release flows directly from this
evidence of 'his great contentation and abstinence', as a
clinching gesture of magnamimity. There then follows the
conferring of his new name, 'Coriolanus'.[10] Shakespeare
delays the incident of the Volscian prisoner until *after*
Martius has received his new name, and creates an entirely

new interest in the question of names, the getting and the losing of them.

Various motives can be imputed to this apparently unpremeditated movement on Martius's part. It is the first time that he fails to see something through. From what we have seen of him so far, it is improbable that he should make such a gesture of magnanimity purely to impress his listeners. As we wonder what moves him here, it is difficult to resist the sense that it has something to do with the new name that he has himself just acquired. It is as if the burden of being under an obligation to the Romans who have given him a new name has created in him the need to displace that burden of obligation on to someone else. But why does he forget the man's name? Is he transferring his own impatience with his new name, projecting his own wish *not to be named* on to this stranger?

How oddly abrupt is the way in which he recalls the memory of this man whom he allowed to use him 'kindly', as he will allow no one to use him in Rome. He will allow Aufidius to use him kindly; perhaps he finds it easier amongst strangers:

> I sometime lay here in Corioles,
> At a poor man's house: he us'd me kindly.
> He cried to me. I saw him prisoner.
> But then Aufidius was within my view,
> And wrath o'erwhelm'd my pity.

(I.ix. 80–4)

It takes the listener a moment to register the sudden change of past tenses between 'he us'd me kindly' and 'He cried to me'. The absence of a grammatical connection makes it seem as if the past were a single undifferentiated time, in which this man's kindness and his cry to Martius followed each other without a break.[11] Martius's memory slurs over the temporal differences between the kindness and the crying and the pity, creating a momentary haven in which men might answer each others' needs, a little world elsewhere and elsewhen. Yet as the image of Aufidius o'erwhelmed him with wrath then, so the flood of weariness o'erwhelms him now: 'My memory is tired'. Martius's memory is a mysterious organ, and its qualities and functionings will come to seem increasingly important as the play progresses.

He certainly remembers Aufidius. But does Aufidius dominate his memory to quite the extent that he dominates Aufidius's? The next brief scene warns us of the ominous power of Aufidius's memory. He is laying up stores for the future, in which the 'embarquements of fury' (I.x. 22) will prove pathetically inadequate. Nor will it only be his own fury against which customs and canons will vainly muster their power of privilege. Martius too will soon be inveighing against 'custom'; Cominius will helplessly invoke the 'canon' against the malice of the tribunes. At the end of the play's first scene, Martius left behind him in Rome the smouldering menace of the plebeians' discontent, awaiting the tribunes' future orchestration. So now as we leave the scenes of 'war' to return to the city and to 'peace', the menace of Aufidius's enmity is impressed on our memories as something that will return to take its revenge in the future. Aufidius dissociates himself from the formal piety professed by everyone else in the play, when he takes the unusual course of swearing 'by th'elements'. (Iago is the only other Shakespearian character to use such an oath, in *Othello*, III.iii. 471.) We get the sense that Martius will haunt Aufidius's every waking and dreaming moment from the uncomfortably literal ring in Aufidius's culminating vow: '. . .would I/Wash my fierce hand in's heart' (I.x. 26–7). This does not sound altogether like a figure of speech.

There is also a barely perceptible effect in Aufidius's finding a new relation to space and time, when he tells the soldiers that he is 'attended at the cypress grove . . . south the city mills', and that he will spur on his journey to the pace of the world (I.x. 30–3). These lines provide an obscure sense of relief in their intimation of a world that contains both cypresses and mills. Aufidius shows a resilience in preparing to accept a new place at the edge of things in which he can learn to adapt himself to the world's 'pace'. This contrasts sharply with Martius, who has no choice but to stand at the centre of things back in Rome, and to have his pace dictated by the world around him. Soon he will be saying that he cannot bring his tongue to such a 'pace' (II.iii. 53).

The great central stretch of the play extends from Martius's triumphal entry into Rome to his humiliated exit—(from Act 2 Scene 1 to Act 4 Scene 3). Much of the dramatic interest here centres on the image of a man who is forced to stand at the centre of a stage that is not of his own choosing, his place and time determined by others. We may increasingly recall the image of his wife, who refused to budge from the place and time she had marked out for herself.

Before Martius enters Rome bearing the name of the enemy city he has conquered, there are two short episodes that prepare us for him. Both of them fashion a new attitude towards 'character', or the apprehension and imagining of character. Up until now the play has been characterised by more or less violent motion, both in the streets of Rome and on the battlefield, a motion 'resolved' first by words (the political decision to grant the tribunate) and by swords (Martius on the battlefield). Now the movement of the play is slowed down and increasingly formalised. Or rather, it becomes a pressing question what 'forms' will be able to control the double energies represented by the needs of the people of Rome and the violent valour represented by Martius.

The scene between Menenius and the tribunes introduces this slower pace. They are waiting for news of the battles, and Menenius turns the talk to the question of 'character'. He sketches an ampler and more familiar view than we have seen so far of the daily life of a city, and two character studies in a recognisably contemporary idiom.[12] Both of these stand at some distance from the individuals they are supposed to represent. The character he creates for himself represents something that is neither quite the way in which he thinks of himself nor quite the way in which other people think of him. It is something between the two, the way in which Menenius would like other people to think of him. His very facility in spinning this image of himself helps him to pre-empt the ways in which other people would choose to describe him. He proposes a bluff image of goodhearted, impulsive conviviality; and a *bluff* is exactly what it is. It is sharply at odds neither with the ways in which he is 'known' by other people nor with the ways in which he thinks and feels about himself. But it is not the whole truth about him, any more than Brutus's attempt to twist this image—'more a perfecter giber at the table than a necessary bencher in the Capitol'—excises the suspicion that it is precisely because Menenius is such a good giber that he *is* a necessary, or at least extremely useful, politician. He presents himself and the tribunes as political cartoons. The tribunes are much more effective and dangerous politicians than his mockery of them as fumblingly self-important clowns makes out, and so is he. And they all know it.

This is the small change of political life, the digressions of political animals flexing their muscles while they wait for the serious business: 'the complex comedy of public behaviour', as Bayley puts it.[13] The serious business is approaching in the shape of Martius, but again there is an important scene of preparation, which goes towards characterising the city which will have to absorb him and into which he will have to settle, again. Or to be exact some aspects of the city, represented by the family gathering of the three women and Menenius. This family is no more united than any family in such a situation, Virgilia's involuntary expressions of anxiety contrasting with Volumnia's manic exultation. Volumnia is already numbering the notches on an icon as she counts the wounds on Martius's body. This is no tender body but a body hardened into a trophy or monument, on which Menenius scores his obscure metonymic fantasy that 'every gash was an enemy's grave'. Volumnia greets the sound of the trumpets with an elevation from prose into verse that is as exhilarating as it is chilling:[14]

> These are the ushers of Martius: before him he carries noise, and behind him he leaves tears:
> Death, that dark spirit, in's nervy arm doth lie,
> Which, being advanc'd, declines, and then men die.
>
> (II.i. 157–60)

The formality of rhyme lends an inhuman serenity to her voice, as the couplet itself advances and declines into eery numbness.

This is the first time that we see Martius together with his family. It is the first of three occasions in the play; the first is a scene of reunion, the second of parting (IV.i) and the third is a scene of reunion *and* parting (V.iii). All of them are public occasions witnessed by others, and on all of them we sense the sharp constraint on the possibility of expressing such personal emotions as these individuals may be presumed to feel for each other.

The constraint can be gauged here by the pressure put on the exclamations 'Oh' and 'Ah'. First there is the 'Oh' with which Martius responds to the nudge from Cominius that points him towards his mother's presence: 'Look, sir, your mother'. 'Oh!' (II.ii. 168). The difficulty this poses for an actor is comparable to the notorious difficulties suffered by the actors playing Lady Macbeth and Malcolm, when they are called on to react in public to the news of Duncan's murder: 'What, in our house?' and 'Oh, by whom?' (*Macbeth*, II.iii. 86, 98). Volumnia in her turn marks the awkwardness of recognising emotional obligations too conflicting for any formulas to ease them off, when she breaks her speech to say, 'But oh, thy wife—'. We cannot know what the exclamation conceals or reveals. It marks, simply, a difficulty or even impossibility about which we can only speculate. The third exclamation, however, is slightly different. The first two 'oh's' are potentially comical in so far as Martius and Volumnia find themselves involuntarily recalled to the relations and obligations of the family grouping—the son to the mother, the mother to her daughter-in-law and her son. But the 'Ah, my dear' with which Martius addresses his wife is a more measured expression of feeling, as near to a tenderness as anything we have heard from him so far in the play. (It is, for what it is worth, the only 'Ah' in the play—and the only time Martius calls anyone 'my dear'.) The tenderness grows out of the apparent formality with which he first hails her, famously, as 'My gracious silence' (II.i. 174). The collectedness of this address is in notable contrast to the fumble of his first words to his mother. Volumnia has just said of her son that 'before him he carries noise, and behind him he leaves tears', but here his wife's tears are before him. It is on his mother's image that he draws when he gently disputes the tact of Virgilia's tears. Her tears are puzzling to a mentality for which triumph and disaster, joy and grief are clearly distinct—the mentality that Volumnia has tried to instil in her son, and in herself. They are also wordlessly prophetic of the tears that lie ahead of Martius.

Martius touches a plaintive note when he says to his mother and wife that he must visit the good patricians, 'Ere in our own house I do shade my head' (II.i. 193). There is little 'shade' in the world of this play. Sicinius has recourse to an obscure image when he says that Martius 'disdains the shadow/ Which he treads on at noon' (I.i. 259–60)—as if Martius were committed to an existence that was all substance and no shadow. 'Our own house' is a place that we never see Martius enjoying in peace with his family. It is ironic that the word 'home' occurs more frequently in this play than in any other of Shakespeare's. But it is significant that the word represents less a place than a direction, more

an adverb than a noun, as in, for example, Martius's
dismissive 'Go get you home, you fragments!' (I.i. 221), or
his violent exhortation 'Mend and charge home' (I.iv. 38),
or Cominius's self-deprecatory 'I cannot speak him home'
(II.ii. 103), or Brutus's conspiratorial 'In this point charge
him home' (III.iii. 1). In these latter three instances the word
'home' is fully figurative, signifying the finality of a
movement that goes right to its mark. The very frequency of
the word serves to suggest the *desire* for a final location that
is never quite attained. This is also the play in which the
word 'Rome' is most often heard,[15] but when Volumnia
does at last voice the rhyme between the two words it is a
desolate finality to which she looks forward:

> So, we will home to Rome
> And die among our neighbours.   (V.iii. 172–3)

'On, to the Capitol', urges Cominius. For the second time
in the play the tribunes are left in possession of the stage at
the end of a public scene. This is the position of power when
men try to plot the future. Brutus's great description of
Martius's passage through the streets of Rome brings out
the sheer exposure of this man, at the centre of everyone's
attention (II.i. 203–19). Where is the centre of the city?
Wherever Martius is. The speech bears comparison with
the description of Bolingbroke's entry into London in
Richard II (V.ii. 7–21), as several critics have pointed out.
And like the conversation of Menenius and the tribunes at
the start of this scene, it would for Shakespeare's first
audiences have slid into the play's representation of the
fictional world of republican Rome the active memory of
comparable triumphant processions through the streets of
contemporary London.

But at the same time the speech has a quite different effect.
For in Brutus's description of the urban masses who gather
in adulation to get a glimpse of this popular celebrity, we
notice that it is quite a different representation of 'the

people' from the one to which we were introduced in the first scene of the play. There is a strong female element in the crowd: 'your prattling nurse', 'the kitchen malkin', 'our veil'd dames'. And there is a strong metonymic propensity in the transformation of particular people into 'tongues' and 'bleared sights' and 'variable complexions'. There is also a religious element provided in the 'seld-shown flamens'. This all adds up to a version of the urban populace radically different from the play's predominant representation of 'the people' as male, political sceptics and activists. Why?

Shakespeare's Roman plays do not present a single or simple image of Rome. Shakespeare and his contemporaries were extremely interested in Roman history and alert to its political implications.[16] In this respect, the differences between republican and imperial Rome were of fundamental importance, and at the time of writing, this play would inevitably have found itself, whether it wished to or not, in close engagement with the contemporary political debate about the values, the institutions and political processes given dramatic embodiment by the history of Rome. Martius will make a ringing appeal to those 'that love the fundamental part of state' (III.i. 150). Whatever he means by this he is not referring to the tribunate. Yet the institution of the tribunate was an essential element in the foundation of the Roman Republic, and there are arguments for reading in this play a sympathy for the ethos of republican Rome capable of overriding the disagreeability of the particular officials who here fill the newly created roles of tribunes.[17] According to such a reading, Martius himself becomes the embodiment of an heroic ethos that in the advancement of the political process has become a dangerous and fundamentally anti-social anachronism. Martius would be comparable to some of the figures who filled the earlier English history plays, in that he represents the glamour of an individualistic ethos that impedes the development of a new collective ethos, cooler, less glamorous, more calculating, but conceivably more humane. And in any case, inevitable. If one presses the comparison, then Martius may seem even more of an anachronism, more radically out of kilter with the developing political necessities of social life than, say, Hotspur.

The attractions of such a reading of the play are that it bolsters our sense of the civic virtues which Martius outrages, and helps to diminish some of the awkward odium which the two particular tribunes seem bound to attract. However this reading is vulnerable to the charge that it underestimates the extent to which Martius is himself a product of the world with which he is out of kilter. If he is an anachronism, he is a living one—always the most dangerous kind. He does not seem much of an anachronism on the battlefield, and even his detractors find it difficult (indeed in the course of the play almost fatal) to pretend that they can utterly do without the kind of brute physical prowess that he represents. There is also a case for seeing in Martius the embodiment of an *idea* of Rome that far surpasses his merely physical triumphs. If he is anti-social, it may be the ignobility of this particular society that creates him in its opposing image.

These questions are stirring in the wake of Brutus's speech. If Martius is an anachronism, the glamour that he reluctantly wields is the product of at least one of his society's needs for such a figure. Brutus can speak these great lines with a grinding exasperation at the public's easy impressibility, at the difficulty of extirpating from his society such ludicrous anachronisms as 'seld-shown flamens' and 'veil'd dames'. What are these Spenserian creatures doing in the modern world? But his exasperation is fired by his knowledge that 'this is what the public wants', a media event, as it were. In a different idiom and context, Octavius Caesar scolds his woe-begone sister for failing to discharge the role she has been given in the theatre of politics. Her return to Rome should have been an orchestrated spectacle:

But you are come
A market-maid to Rome, and have prevented
The ostentation of our love, . . .
                        We should have met you
By sea and land, supplying every stage
With an augmented greeting.

(*Antony and Cleopatra*, III.vi. 50–5).

Caesar knows the value, indeed the necessity, of self-advertisement.

The tribunes in *Coriolanus* are experts in what is now known as 'the media', and beneath its indignation Brutus's speech carries a rueful admiration for the sheer spontaneity of this great, unorchestrated public occasion. If only the tribunes could have got their hands on it; their time will come. The admiration creeps slily into Brutus's final lines, which suggest that he is not immune to the pull of the image he reluctantly utters:

Such a pother,
As if that whatsoever god who leads him
Were slily crept into his human powers,
And gave him graceful posture.

(II.i. 216–19)

It is something for Brutus to admit that a god does lead Martius, however throwaway the 'whatsoever' may be, and however typical of him to imagine that a god would have to creep *slily* into Martius.

Yet while the lines inadvertently characterise Brutus himself, they also carry a pathos that is independent of the speaker, in that they project an image of Martius as a man taken unawares by a force that enters into him. There is a moment in *Twelfth Night* when Olivia tenderly wonders to herself—'Even so quickly may one catch the plague?'

Methinks I feel this youth's perfections
With an invisible and subtle stealth
To creep in at mine eyes. Well, let it be.

(I.v. 279–82)

Many of the most characteristic effects in *Coriolanus* are
achieved by 'an invisible and subtle stealth'. Philip
Brockbank draws shrewdly on the word Shakespeare puts
into Brutus's mouth, when he reflects on the hidden inner
changes that will overtake Martius at the play's climax. Of
Martius's defiant, plaintive words to Aufidius, 'It is no little
thing to make/Mine eyes to sweat compassion', Brockbank
observes, 'Shakespeare seems slily to transpose into human
ordeal Plutarch's marvellings about stone images that seem
to "sweat or weep" in Roman temples'.[18] The human
ordeals that this play represents are certainly painful, yet
there is something oddly comical in the permeability of the
obdurate character that stands so grudgingly at its centre.
We catch a whiff of this comedy at one or more removes,
when we imagine Martius being crept into through the eyes
of a man into whose own imagination Martius has himself
slily crept.

Martius has been driven 'On, to the Capitol', and we are
prepared for some culminating ceremony that will clinch
what Volumnia has called 'the buildings of her fancy', the
supreme acclamation of which the Roman state is capable.
What *is* the ceremony that would serve to clinch
Volumnia's dream? It is split between the formal approval
which the Senate can provide and the no less necessary
approval of the people. This split is mirrored in the division
of place, between the Capitol and the market-place. Martius
must 'stand' in both of these places to be judged and
approved. There are two ceremonies required: for the first
of these Martius extraordinarily absents himself, so as not
to hear the oration with which Cominius ratifies his deeds.
But for the second, his physical presence, much as he would
like to withhold or disguise it, is *de rigueur*. Cominius

recomposes the deeds he has accomplished in the past, while the voices of the people have to approve the graven image of those deeds in the physical signs of his wounded, triumphant body. This latter ceremony constitutes a ritual humiliation to balance Cominius's ritual praise.

In both of these scenes he has to stand to be judged; yet this is just what he cannot stand. He cannot treat his humiliation as a ritual in which he plays a nominal role. He must offer his body as a sign to be read and re-uttered by the words of others. But he cannot accept that his body is a sign available for others to read, for in reading it they are being granted the right of judgement over it. He can make no separation between himself and his body; he cannot wear his body as an outward role, as Menenius can, for instance. If others are granted the right to approve what he shows them, then this means that they have the power to disapprove.

It is not merely that he cannot bring himself to honour the right of the people to pass judgement on him. His impatience with the Senate's need to judge him is almost as raw, though the presence of the tribunes amidst the patricians certainly contributes to that rawness—as they take pains to ensure. The courtesy of Brutus's impudence is wonderfully comical: 'Sir, I hope/My words disbench'd you not?' (II.ii. 70–1). We have heard Martius say that he is grieved even by his mother's praises, and we sense that this man may find something repellent in the prospect of *anyone* judging him. It is the act of judgement itself that grieves him rather than the particular incompetence of any individual judge or jury. The fact that in this instance both kinds of jury, the Senate and the people, seem bound to issue a favourable verdict is neither here nor there. No trophy they could award him could compensate for the damage he feels to be inherent in the process of judgement.

It is not only to the man to be judged to whom we attend; it is also to the judges. Here the preparatory exchanges between the two Officers in the Capitol and between the plebeians in the market-place alert us to the difficulties in the processes of judgement for all concerned. We remember the uneasy elation in the First Citizen's voice at the start of the play, when he cried prematurely, 'A verdict'—a 'true word'. The innumerable preparatory and linking scenes give real substance to the problem of explaining and interpreting and judging Martius, a problem that is itself one of the play's main subjects. Cominius's formal oration is a grand attempt to still and solidify both the subject of his speech, 'Coriolanus', and the process of interpretation itself.

Cominius's speech has a wonderful trajectory to it. He begins with an avowal of inadequacy and a hesitation over the terms to which he appeals, that may or may not be purely formal:

> It is held
> That valour is the chiefest virtue and
> Most dignifies the haver; if it be, . . .

(II.ii. 83–5)

There is a mounting horror in the movement of his speech. It starts from an uneasy facetiousness in the image of the fledgeling warrior, fronting the 'bristled lips' with his 'Amazonian chin', a metonymy that displaces attention from an integral whole to a representative part. Such metonymies are always potentially comical: they are an essential ingredient in the cartoonist's repertoire. But they can also be menacing in their cumulative effect. *Does* the part represent a whole, or does it perhaps take on an independent life of its own—a member that no longer has a body to belong to?[19]

The Amazonian chin may be relatively harmless (though the 'Amazonian' is never entirely devoid of menace). But the figures by which Cominius tries to do justice to Martius and his feats become progressively monstrous. This confirms Martius's fear that his deeds would be 'monstered', though perhaps not in the sense that he intended. Does Cominius realise what he is doing, as he draws with ever-increasing flourishes the lineaments of a monstrous, supernatural force?

> his sword, death's stamp,
> Where it did mark, it took; from face to foot
> He was a thing of blood, whose every motion
> Was tim'd with dying cries: alone he enter'd
> The mortal gate of th'city, which he painted
> With shunless destiny, aidless came off,
> And with a sudden reinforcement struck
> Corioles like a planet.
>
>   (II.ii. 107–14)

There is certainly horror in his speech, but there is room for readers and audiences and actors to find varying degrees of consciousness behind or within the words. One can suppose Cominius oblivious to the horror of his own words; he may find a grim satisfaction in them, or perhaps even a sociable satisfaction in measuring up to the challenge to produce, in front of his peers, a speech equal to the occasion, a satisfaction that could be clinched by the Senate's formal applause. There is no evidence in the text that the Senate find anything disturbing in the images he wields. Menenius nods approvingly, with direct reference to the subject of the speech, but also indirectly to its speaker: 'Worthy man'.

However, it is also possible to imagine in Cominius a consciousness of the implications of what he is saying, a consciousness obscure or overt or rising only to be suppressed.[20] There is certainly something that asks for explanation in the way that Cominius's speech comes to an end. Cominius has not quite finished when Menenius and the first Senator intervene to voice their approval. Perhaps Cominius has thrown himself so forcefully into the spirit of his speech that he too needs to 'ease his breast with panting', as he has described Martius doing (II.ii. 122). But in the six further lines with which he returns to conclude his oration,

he touches a note of remonstrance that recalls the
awkwardness of that scene on the battlefield, when Martius
scorned Cominius's ability to reward him.

> Our spoils he kick'd at,
> And look'd upon things precious as they were
> The common muck of the world.
>
> (II.ii. 124–6)

This is something other than the 'noble carelessness' to
which the Second Officer alluded, and although there may
be admiration there must also be at the very least some
bewilderment in Cominius's recollection of such imperious
disparagement.

Martius's relations with the other patricians leave some
room for interpretation. Shakespeare plays down the point
that Plutarch makes of the divisions that Martius causes
among the patricians, and in particular of the popularity
which he enjoys with the younger nobility. (A bare hint of
this survives in the stage-direction at the head of Act 4 Scene
1 which refers to 'the young Nobility of Rome'). But there is
an important problem here, the nature of which can be
gauged by this effort to resolve it in Kenneth Tynan's
description of Olivier's 1959 performance:

> Olivier understands that Coriolanus is not an aristocrat;
> he is a professional soldier, a *Junker*, if you like,
> reminiscent in many ways of General de Gaulle—a
> rejected military saviour who returns, after a long and
> bodeful silence, with an army at his back. Fully aware of
> the gap between Coriolanus and the patricians he is
> serving, Olivier uses it to gain for the man an astounding
> degree of sympathy.[21]

It is clearly a simplification—albeit a powerful and
theatrically successful one—to distinguish Martius so
sharply from the 'aristocrats' by making him a professional

soldier. The play certainly means him to be both an aristocrat and a soldier.

It is not Tynan's fault nor that of the production he is describing that all interpretations of the play are bound to be coloured by contemporary images of aristocrats and soldiers and military saviours, and the rhetoric that surrounds them. But to make Martius a *professional* soldier is to call attention to a problem that is one of the play's own subjects: the relation between those martial virtues that are necessary and valuable out there in the field, and the city or state back home which they serve. When there is a clearly understood division between city and field, and employers and servants, then you can have professional soldiers who make the business of war their living, whether they serve one state or many. Othello is a professional soldier and his play is at least partly the tragedy of a professional soldier. He has been at home all his life out there in the field with other professionals like Iago. For the first time in his life he has taken a break from work and gone 'home' to Venice. It is the conflict between these different homes, the feelings and beliefs about being at home and having a home, that tears him apart. But the Venice of that play is entirely different from the Rome of this. It is an imperial power with far-flung possessions and trade routes which need to be secured by the services of professional soldiers like Othello. The case is similar with the imperial Rome of *Antony and Cleopatra*, though it is complicated by the civil war that is fought across its vast spaces. The play is none the less thronged by characters whom it is reasonable to describe as 'professional soldiers'—men such as Ventidius and Silius in Syria (III.i.), Canidius and the anonymous soldier who begs Antony not to fight by sea at Actium (III.vii.).

But the early republican Rome of *Coriolanus* cannot afford the luxury of a professional class of soldiers or a standing army. Shakespeare scarcely needs to insist on the implications spelt out by the Plutarch source, that the wars take people away from the land and from the production of food. The problem which Martius sets Rome is not just a matter of his personal temperament. It is inherent in the very condition of a small city-state that has not reached the stage at which it can afford to make clear distinctions between war and peace, or the manpower that can be devoted to these separate spheres. It is the same people who must serve the city in its daily needs and who must serve it out there in the field. The patricians pride themselves on the 'distinctions' which uphold their city, and Cominius confesses to a revealing fear when he envisages the chaos that will 'bury all which yet distinctly ranges' (III.i. 204). But the need to insist on distinction is built on the fear of its absence, and this fear is written into the very constitution of Rome. It is a city only in the most embryonic and vulnerable phase of development, in which it has yet to secure its own frontiers. Martius is, as it were, the concentrated symptom of this collective problem in the city's history, its need for the professional soldier whom it cannot afford to keep permanently out in the field, and for whose re-entry into its inner spaces it fails to provide the necessary rites of passage. Indeed, when Martius returns in triumph to Rome he is swept towards the summit and centre of civil power before he barely has time to draw breath or, as he puts it, 'to shade his head'.

There is a level at which the history of his personal passage and its disastrous consequences can be taken to epitomise a general problem in the developing history of the city—not just the particular Rome of the early Republic, or of any literal, material *place*, but of 'the city' as a collective idea or even a state of consciousness. Gail Kern Paster writes:

Like Coriolanus, who is both an historical personage reasonably well known to an educated Elizabethan and the embodiment of a heroic type, the city which casts him out is both the historical Rome of the early Republic and the 'City,' that symbol of the human community bound togethe by the same gods, heroes, laws, customs, buildings, and walls.[22]

At this level of abstraction the play can be taken to represent the difficulties encountered in an expanding consciousness of human relations, or even the difficult fact of diversity itself in the multiple relations, public and private, political, social, emotional and intellectual, that are created and broken by the demands of collective living.

Meanwhile, Martius is on his way to the market-place, to discharge 'the custom of request'.

·3·

'Most sweet voices!'

Martius has still not found time to shade his head before he is swept off to the market-place. The citizens who gather expectantly are the unpredictable element in this apparently inexorable political process. The Third Citizen characterises this irresolution with comically unabashed candour when he imagines their wits flying to all points of the compass, failing to keep a 'course of one consent'. Or, as one of the tribunes tetchily remarks, they show a 'childish friendliness' in their tentative 'kindness' towards Martius, their goodwill to think well of him and his intentions towards them, their wish to play their part in this ceremony properly. Such ceremonies depend on goodwill, on a graciousness on the part of the actors. We may recall the 'gracious posture' which Brutus acknowledged in Martius. Everyone knows that Martius's progress to the heights of public acclaim is unimpedable, if he just falls into a gracious posture and allows the 'grace' with which his deeds have endowed him to have its way.

We have seen enough of him by now to realise how excruciating he must find the prospect of playing a part in what he feels to be an empty charade. It is not that he *asks* for sympathy. It is rare indeed for this man to be caught showing anything other than a carelessness, noble or otherwise, at what anyone else may think or feel about him.

As for the people of Rome—'Think upon me? Hang 'em!'
(II.iii. 58). So far from enjoying the freedom of his entry into
other people's imaginations, thoughts and feelings, he
recoils from the prospect of laying his very self open to
abuse. An audience, literal or figurative, is what he cannot
stand the idea of.

'Why in this wolvish toge should I stand here . . .?' (II.iii.
114) 'Standing' turns out to be an important activity and
idea in the play, both on its own and with various
prepositions: 'stand in', 'stand upon', 'stand for', 'stand
with', 'stand to'. In so far as Martius's capacity for relentless
motion allows him to 'stand', his happiest posture is one of
standing fast, preferably *against* other people. Two of his
most memorable uses of the word will be inspired by the
climactic assault made on him by his own family. As his
mother approaches he will gird himself up to

> stand
> As if a man were author of himself
> And knew no other kin.
>
> (V.iii. 35–7)

In his own young son he sees a grand epitome of himself, and
he blesses the boy's future with the generous imagination of
his own proud independence, 'like a great sea-mark standing
every flaw' (V.iii. 74).

But standing *for* things (in both senses) is what he finds
abhorrent. 'I won't stand for it!' might well be his motto. He
does not care to stand for praise, the consulship, the
people's voices—any activity that would involve conceding
that he is playing or representing a 'part' rather than a whole:
'You have put me now to such a part which never/I shall
discharge to th'life' (III.ii. 105–6), he will say to his mother.
And his wife will move him to concede that 'Like a dull
actor now/I have forgot my part . . .' (V.iii. 40–1). A 'part' is
a role and a role is not a whole. This helps to explain the
deep suspicion, amounting at times to hatred, that Martius

seems to feel towards language itself, which is of its very nature a representative medium.[1]

It may also suggest some of the peculiar difficulties facing an actor who has to play the part of a man for whom playing a part seems a denial of his very being. Any actor who plays this role should be promptly compensated by a spell as Richard III. Bayley notes the difficulty facing the actor, that his 'capacity to make the part a "moving" one is alienated by the nature of the part'. But he helpfully overstates the difficulty by going on to say:

> Coriolanus, and Timon who follows him [*sic*], are paradoxical creations, heroes whose sense of themselves is so determined as to preclude any of the play of human variety and awareness which a good actor conducts and reveals, and transmits to the audience in the form of emotional depth and uncertainty.[2]

What—'so determined as to preclude *any* of the play'? This suggests both the difficulty but also the attraction in the role, that the actor needs to seek out the frailty within the iron resolution. What may seem to the reader a difficulty or even impossibility will seem to the actor and director a challenge and an opportunity. Granville-Barker remarks that in his later plays 'Shakespeare has come to demanding more of his actors, and to giving them more—though it may be less ostensible—opportunity'.[3] He calls particular attention to the power of 'the dynamic phrase', of gesture and silence and reticence.

Martius has a sense of humour but the idea of making a fool of himself does not appeal to him. At the climax of the play he will at last bare a tenderness to this sense of his own risibility, when he imagines the gods' *laughing* at him. For the other human beings in the play he is no laughing matter. Such 'mirth' as we hear in Rome is behind his back (Valeria and Volumnia in Act 1 Scene 3, Menenius, the tribunes). There is a nervous strain in the pleasure expressed in his presence even by the men he gets on well with—Cominius, Menenius, Aufidius. Significantly enough, the only occasions on which he shares anything like real mirth are in his exchanges with Titus Lartius before the siege of Corioles (I.iv. 1–7), and with Cominius before his entry into the field-battle (I.vi. 25–32). There he is really relaxed. Elsewhere his mirth is savage rather than genial, something to be brandished in the face of his enemies rather than savoured with his friends. But the moments at which we hear this savage mirth can strangely recapture this quality of relaxation, when he breathes freely, happily. They are the moments of supreme self-assertion in the teeth of the howling mob—'You common cry of curs . . .' (III.iii. 120ff.), or in the teeth of the Volscians at the end—'Cut me to pieces, Volsces . . .' (V.vi. 111ff.). It is a relaxation that comes with the moments of supreme danger, when his power is wrenched up to the highest.

Those are the moments when, paradoxically, he can feel safe. But when the risks are less obvious and the means of facing them less certain, his dignity becomes almost touchingly precarious. The precariousness is not touching to those around him of course; they are mostly too scared of him to notice or care. But it may touch the less threatened spectator, as it touched Hazlitt when he came to consider the effect of Kemble's statuesque playing of the role: 'Kemble's supercilious airs and *nonchalance* remind one of the unaccountable abstracted air, the contracted eyebrows and suspended chin of a man who is just going to sneeze'.[4] A man is not the author of himself when he is just going to sneeze, and Hazlitt's comment is in its oblique fashion a wonderfully adroit observation on the character Kemble played so famously. In the end Martius does more than sneeze; he weeps—or as he puts it, with a typically rueful awkwardness, he 'sweats compassion'. Long before he does so, an audience may be made to feel towards him the kind of tender malice inspired by the sight of someone who needs to sneeze.

In the market-place his sense of his own dignity is under extreme siege. 'What must I say?': he really does not know. There is a striking sense of relief when for a moment the plebeians' assault abates, and he is left alone on stage. At such a moment we are likely to feel that as readers or audience in the theatre we constitute a superior, more intimate audience in whom the central figure may wish to, may even in some obscure way be *bound* to confide. Of course the people who constitute an audience within the world of his play are inadequate, gross and importunate and threatening. But we who stand outside the world of the play, we do not threaten, or beg, or plead with him, we do not *expect* things of him, do we? Surely he will, in such a moment of relief from the demands of his own world reach out to us, his more kindly, impartial auditors? And in that reaching out, he will be reaching in, to reveal that deeper self which he conceals from others immediately around him. We will be that inner audience, privileged to hear the dialogue of a man with his self, a dialogue that is denied to others.

'Most sweet voices!' Martius does have a brief speech here (II.iii. 111–23), though the absence of self-reflection in it leads commentators to deny that it is a 'real' soliloquy. For a character whose singleness is made so much of in the play it is notable that we only find him alone on this and one other later occasion, before Aufidius's house in Antium. It is often said that at ·these moments Martius reveals his essential limitations, his lack of inwardness. He is, it is endlessly repeated, the least eloquent of Shakespeare's tragic figures. Now Hamlet—*there* is someone who knows how to talk when he gets the stage to himself. Danson usefully spells out some of the presuppositions behind this position, when he sketches a large argument about the role of language in Shakespearian tragedy. He is setting things in motion with Titus Andronicus:

All of Shakespeare's tragic heroes share with Titus a self-expressive task: as they suffer greatly they must speak

greatly, their eloquence matching their pain. But
everywhere, although not so obviously as in *Titus*, the
great difficulty of that task is apparent. . . . What we
watch in Shakespearian tragedy, then, is not only man
speaking, but man trying to speak, trying to create the
language that can denote him truly.[5]

This last emphasis is indeed important: on man trying to
speak, trying to create a true language. But one may wonder
where the imperative comes from in Danson's contention
that 'as they suffer greatly they *must* speak greatly'. Why
must they? Outside artistic representations great suffering
rarely coincides with great eloquence, and it is too easy to
suppose that this is exactly the dream which tragic art fulfils.
Opera can provide such unscrupulous dreams, but for that
very reason it usually takes us beyond the domain of
tragedy. Danson is right to speak of the 'great difficulty' of
the task, but the terms of the task are more complicated than
he allows. Is the imperative which bids great sufferers try to
speak, a compulsion, a need or a duty? Do they owe it to
themselves or do they owe it to others? Is there some sort of
social obligation in this task of self-expression, to put their
sufferings into words?

These are particularly important questions in this play,
and Danson's argument is useful in raising them. One of the
play's central difficulties and interests lies in the problem of
'self-expression', and the resentment provoked by the
central character's failure to meet his supposed obligations
towards the audience. Does he have a self to express at all? It
is possible to believe that he does not, and that the play
assaults the very notion of an essential self.[6] It is also
possible to believe that he *does* have an essential self and that
there is something honourable in his keeping it to himself.
These and other readings are evidently possible, and one of
the play's claims to greatness consists in the provocation
and hospitality that it offers to divergent beliefs about the
self.

But it is important not to isolate the problem of Martius's self from the world in which it is necessarily placed. Much of the difficulty that tragic characters find in 'trying to speak' is that the language they have to wield can never be their personal property. The 'self' that they are trying to express is already at least partly expressed by the language they have to use. They do not just speak; they are also spoken by others. This aspect of the 'task' is represented in *Coriolanus* with more severity and consistency than in any other Shakespearian tragedy. Martius may or may not have a self of his own; he certainly has selves which are the product of other people's thoughts and feelings and imaginings. His problem may be to resist the invasion of this 'other' language, the otherness of language, rather than to create a new language that will denote him truly. *He* does not seem to believe that he needs to create a new language: he already speaks his own language—if only other people will leave him alone. But other people cannot leave him alone, even if they wanted to. In this fundamental respect he is no different from all other Shakespearian tragic characters—in that in their different ways, their tragedies are always also other people's.

Martius's soliloquy in the market-place begins to raise such issues as these, but it is important to hear the speech in its context. It is hardly Martius's fault that this is no leisurely act of self-communion. It is certainly notable that, as Cantor points out, this speech is 'the only sustained passage of rhymed verse in the entire play'. But the inference he draws is unwarrantably severe: 'Instead of trying to reflect, Coriolanus merely spouts sententious maxims in rhyme, audibly forcing himself to recall lessons he has learned by rote.'[7] One might more sympathetically interpret the recourse to lessons that he has learnt by rote as a necessary tactic to protect his feelings of outrage at a viciously demeaning situation. Nor need one conclude that all lessons that are learnt by rote remain entirely without inner meaning for the pupil. In other words, Martius may

take the sententious maxims he 'spouts' either more
seriously or less seriously than the critic who is intent on
finding an exact equation between expression and feeling.
There is no means of telling—and therefore room for the
actor.

In fact Martius's speech is more interesting than Cantor
makes out, for he cannot have learnt all of its maxims by
rote. Though it may begin woodenly, the rhythm of thought
changes, as Martius discovers an idea which is starkly at
odds with the whole notion of received wisdom:

> What custom wills, in all things should we do't,
> The dust on antique time would lie unswept
> And mountainous error be too highly heap'd
> For truth to o'erpeer.
>
> (II.iii. 117–20)

We may still hear the formality of rhyme, but a cumulative
energy carries the thought of 'mountainous error' over the
pattern that tries to contain it. The movement of the
sentence mimes the action it describes, by 'heaping' words
too highly for their thought to be contained. For Martius is
here, however unwittingly, setting himself up as an
'innovator', a role in which the tribunes will smack their lips
at the prospect of fixing him. Martius may think of himself,
and be thought of by others, as the staunch advocate of
things as they are and always have been, of a customary
patrician order under siege from a low democratic age. But
at this particular moment he is at odds with 'custom'. In
disparaging this specific custom, he calls into question the
whole role of ceremony in sustaining a social order. What
appals him is the whole *theatrical* basis of public and
political life.

Yet we should note the difficulty of deciding how
pondered, if at all, are his words about 'custom'. His
thought itself suggests the possibility of seeing through the
fallacies of 'customary' behaviour. But the way in which it is

expressed conveys an almost comical pathos in the difficulty of overturning the sheer weight of habit represented by 'mountainous error'. We may later recall this image of plucky truth pitting its efforts against mountainous error, when Martius imagines the weight and height of his mother bearing down on him. In the face of that great image of custom, his mother, he imagines her not as mountainous error but as Olympus—and himself as a molehill (V.iii. 30).

What is it that he wants? He wants it to be over, the hideous fiction in which he is caught. Hence the sudden lameness with which he ends this moment of vexed but momentarily visionary reverie:

> I am half through,
> The one part suffer'd, the other will I do.
>
> (II.iii. 22–3)

The most striking aspect of the rest of this scene is its sheer protractedness. Assisted by the Third Citizen's impressive powers of mimicry (II.iii. 164–71), the tribunes quickly seize on the people's discomfort with Martius's behaviour. But it is surprising that they spend so much time in going over what the plebeians ought to have said, and in rehearsing them in what they have to say now. This is partly a question of dramatic rhythm. The sense of slight delay increases an audience's impatience to reach the scenes of violent confrontation which surely lie ahead. This is true in general of the play, that the timing of the great scenes of confrontation depends for its effect on the cunningly paced delays provided by intermediate scenes. But there is also dramatic point to the sense we get of the sheer effort required by the tribunes to harness the irresolute energy embodied in the people. The people are *not* naturally disposed towards violence or insurrection or confrontation. They have to be carefully primed. In this respect we will discover an unexpectedly convincing resemblance between them and Martius himself: they are both children when it comes to the manipulation of public performances. The tribunes rehearse their performers here as Menenius and Volumnia will later rehearse Martius (III.ii.).[8]

There is an importat irresolution in the location of the three scenes of Act 3. In fact this next scene must take place somewhere between the Capitol and the market-place, the twin but divided centres of power and decision. In the previous scene first Martius and then the people have exited in the direction of the Capitol. Now we see Martius entering with 'all the Gentry', and speaking on the move to Titus Lartius and others about the prospect of further wars with the Volsces. Where is Martius going to? It is only on the entrance of the tribunes barring his way, that it turns out that he is on his way to the market-place—again. The reader of North's Plutarch will have known that this was the occasion on which Martius's behaviour outraged the people. In North, Martius does not turn a hair about showing his wounds, and it is only when he turns up in the market-place on the day of election itself 'with great pompe, accompanied with all the Senate, and the whole Nobilitie of the cittie about him', that the people turn against him.[9]

It is in the teeth of this obstruction to his onward passage that Martius is spurred into enunciating an idea of what he stands for. It is an idea of Rome as an ideal state in which men would speak and act with one voice, in which speech would be action and action words. This belief in the integrity of a state is for him at once personal and public: he can make no distinction between the two. Singleness is his dream of being, both for himself and for the state which he serves. Within this latter state, the city of Rome, the differences between beings must be subordinated to the service of the whole, in a co-ordination analogous to the articulation of a healthy body. That co-ordination and integrity is precious for its readiness to be pitted against the enemy other, which lies outside in a state of permanent antagonism. The admission of otherness or dissent *within* the single body would be a betrayal of that body's primary purpose and value.

As we listen to the great ringing speeches in which he denounces the various betrayals of this ideal (III.i. 90–111, 118–38, 139–60), we may get the sense of a double exposure, of an ideal vision struggling for expression against the realities of common life. We can trace the pathos of this struggle in the figures of speech through which Martius, his enemies and friends strive to persuade themselves and each other of the reality of their claims. There are the various figures relating to the body, which from the start of the play have signalled the effort to control and project interpretations of relationship, of loyalties and obligations. At times these figures threaten to take on a life of their own, in a drama of their own. For Martius the tribunes are the 'mouths' of the common people. At the climax of the appeal to his fellow-patricians the tribunes become 'the multitudinous tongue' (III.i. 155). The people themselves are a voiceless belly, a 'bosom multiplied' (III.i. 130), whose subordination to the higher elements of the body politic is put in jeopardy by their being granted a voice, a mouth, a tongue. For Martius, it is not the patricians who are the belly, but the common people—a more orthodox view of the body's parts and their hierarchical relation than Menenius's fable offered.

Martius is outraged by the people's claims both to food and to speech; the two claims are related. Food, he argues, is something which must be deserved, which should not be given freely, 'gratis'. Here we begin to realise quite how much of Martius's animus is focused on the role of the mouth and tongue in his projected image of the body: 'at once pluck out/The multitudinous tongue', he cries (III.i. 154–5). Martius indulges in a peculiar grammatical violence by making the singular 'tongue' consort so improbably with the plurality of its adjective (unlike Macbeth's famous 'multitudinous seas'). The mouth and tongue are both the means by which food passes into the body, and the means by which speech passes out. In both cases Martius takes the severe line that both food and speech must first be deserved before they can be ingested or uttered.

What *is* at the roots of this enmity between Martius and his 'sworn brother the people', as he ironically calls them in the market-place (II.iii. 95)? One could take a cue from this to suggest that Martius shows something of the severity of an elder brother towards the younger siblings whom mother Rome pampers with the free food that they ought first to deserve.[10] His mother has certainly not pampered him with the milk of human kindness. There is an obscure sense of rivalry in Martius's feelings about the plebeians that seems to have something to do with charity and gratitude, and justice and service. Everyone should deserve what they get. If there is virtue in Martius's vision of the city, it is partly that he sees the reality of the enmity in the differences between people, and insists on announcing them. He unmasks the hypocrisy that would seek to minimise them or keep them hidden. His idea of the city leaves no room for charity.

Lionel Trilling makes a striking connection between speaking and eating in the course of some large reflections on the differences between English and American literature. He is pondering the contrast between *Kim* and *Huckleberry Finn*, and he goes on to argue for the fundamentally anti-social inspiration of the literature to which Twain's book belongs. In Thoreau, for instance, the suspicion of organised society amounts, Trilling says, to a horror of 'the human condition in general': 'He loathed the necessities of ordinary life, thought it a desecration of the divinity of language that it must be uttered by the mouth which also serves the animal necessity of eating'.[11] This idea of a primary loathing comes interestingly close to something we may read into Martius's 'psychology', a loathing that would make him apt for migration into the ethos of American literature (as Trilling imagines it) and its founding conviction that 'virtue lies in alienation from society'.[12] But

Martius would need a lot of education before he could speak the same language as Thoreau. The idea that language might possess or manifest a *divinity* seems beyond Martius and the world by which he is circumscribed. He is rigorously bound by the necessities of ordinary life which include both eating and speaking: there is no world elsewhere.

Yet in Martius's speech there are tantalising hints of the vision of an ideal state, and the question of Martius's own hold on these hints is an important one. The problem that Martius poses the audience or reader reaches a particularly sharp focus at the climax of his first great speech of appeal to the patricians: 'O good but most unwise patricians' (III.i. 90):

> and my soul aches
> To know, when two authorities are up,
> Neither supreme, how soon confusion
> May enter 'twixt the gap of both, and take
> The one by th'other.
>
> (III.i. 107–11)

Several critics have remarked on the heartfelt quality of these lines. A. P. Rossiter goes so far as to say that they expose Shakespeare's own feelings: 'I cannot doubt that those lines are heartfélt. They are (for once) what William Shakespeare thought—in 1607'. Our personal feelings about Martius's personality are neither here nor there, Rossiter argues: the fact is that his political convictions, as expressed in this speech, are *right*.[13] Vickers writes with more circumspection about Martius's real political insight—an insight which has perhaps grown under stress—and calls the speech 'an impressive diagnosis of what social discord could do to Rome'. He notes Martius's distance from the other patricians and describes him as 'the only man of the patrician class who has a grasp of the total political situation'.[14]

Is 'grasp' the right word? Martius seems to be grasping *at*
and *for* the enunciation of an idea because he is himself in the
grasp of such violent feelings and such a violent political
situation. J. C. F. Littlewood states the audience's difficulty
with admirable precision when he asks, 'Who can assign the
proportions of the elements that make up that ache in his
soul?'[15] Is Martius moved at once by instinct and by
principle, or moved by instinct *into* principle, or moved by
principle that is merely corroborated by instinct? Rabkin
puts the problem with a pleasant understatement, when he
writes of Martius's idea of honour: 'He believes in honor as
a principle, but perhaps he does so because he has to'.[16]
Such a line of thought can lead to the ominous conclusion
that principles are only held by virtue of psychological
needs, or even more darkly, that they are only the products
of such needs. Rabkin accepts that the play leads to this
conclusion:

> It is Shakespeare's demonstration of the dominance of the
> character over what we would like to be, of the priority of
> personality over principle in the motivation of human
> action, that brings this play as close to being a depressing
> experience as any tragedy of Shakespeare ever gets.[17]

But to speak confidently of the *priority* of personality to
principle is to resolve the play's difficulty—and its
excitement. Littlewood argues that the play's excitement
does dissolve indeed in its latter stages precisely because it
abandons the intense embroilment of personality and
principle that dominates the first part of the play.[18]

Martius launches himself into figures of speech with an
abandon that is as exhilarating as it is terrifying. Around
him the other patricians try to limit its damage and the
tribunes try to capitalise on it. Menenius is the one who
seems most aware of the menacing infirmity of language. He
tries desperately to wield the figures of speech that might
temper the rage that threatens to 'unbuild the city'. There is

an impressive conflation in his simultaneous appeal to figures of paternal and maternal power, to the image of animal cannibalism and the mysterious authority of 'Jove's own book':

> Now the good gods forbid
> That our renowned Rome, whose gratitude
> Towards her deserved children is enroll'd
> In Jove's own book, like an unnatural dam
> Should now eat up her own!
>
> (III.i. 287–91)

But a few lines later his words reveal how far the passions that he is trying to ground are careering out of control. We may have been struck at the time by the oddity of Martius's reference to Corioles being held 'like a fawning greyhound in the leash' (I.vi. 38). Rome is turning out to be a wilder animal and it is breaking free of all its leashes:

> This tiger-footed rage, when it shall find
> The harm of unscann'd swiftness will, too late,
> Tie leaden pounds to's heels.
>
> (III.i. 309–11)

It is a characteristic resort in this play to displace the sense of agency onto something which is recognisably a part or a quality that seeks to stand for an absent whole. But here as elsewhere the quality onto which agency is displaced threatens to assume a life of its own. Menenius is warning his listeners that they will regret their anger, but the human agents are entirely displaced so that it is the 'rage' that does the finding out and the tying of leaden pounds to ''s' (his own?) heels. Menenius's figure predicts a process whose course will on the way it takes irrespective of the agents who try to affect it, or surrender their responsibility to try.

At this point the play has wrenched up its power to the

highest, and it is a proper moment to consider more broadly
some of its political issues. The problem that Martius poses
cannot be dissociated from the collective political context
represented within the play; but this problem and context
are also embroiled with problematic contexts *outside* the
play, both the context in which the play was first written and
those in which it is now produced and read. It is important
to see the ways in which the play incites and resists
interpretation, thus making possible a diversity of readings,
and ensuring its continued dramatic vitality.

Take the other patricians, for example. It is possible to see
them as pusillanimous liberals without the guts to stand up
for what they believe in, or what they ought to believe in if
they really shared Martius's vision of Rome as a true society
based on virtue. According to this line of thought, they
deserve Martius's contempt almost as much as the
plebeians.[19] It is possible to hear in some of Cominius's later
speeches a shame at their failure to support Martius.

But if the patricians are to be accused of a failure of nerve,
one might well convict them of a failure to resist the
lawlessness represented both by Martius and by the
tribunes, rather than reproach them for their failure to rally
round Martius. One might say that they fail sufficiently to
dissociate themselves from Martius's rallying cry. They
have failed to discipline one of their own number, to
educate him into an ïdea of civility that would honour the
principle of divided authority in the state. As it is, their
failure to back Martius may seem no less like an
embarrassed recognition of his real political differences
from them than a shameful betrayal of a shared ideal.

Empson lends some support to this position, when he
brings his usual common sense to bear on Martius's later
complaints about their failure to follow his lead:

he tells Aufidius, after his grizzling in exile, that the other
aristocrats ratted on him when he was banished . . . .
They backed him as far as they could without bringing on

civil war; he should not have expected them to abandon Rome for him.[20]

If the patricians are to blame for betraying Martius, it may be because they have fostered the catastrophically mythic delusions of his stature to which in due course he falls a prey. It is part of Empson's point here that it is the myth of his supernatural prowess that encourages Martius in 'the fatal thought that he has been wronged'.[21] He has grown into believing that he was above the law—like the Lear who mutters the belated discovery, 'They told me I was everything; 'tis a lie—I am not ague-proof' (*King Lear*, IV.vi. 104–5).

What 'law'? There is, we begin to realise, a whole set of terms to do with law, authority and decision that have been set in motion by the very opening words of the play: 'Before we *proceed* any further'. This word had a legal or quasi-legal ring to it, to which Menenius now appeals with some desperation, when he says, 'Proceed by process' (III.i. 311). But what *is* the process, the legal or political or social process that could satisfactorily 'resolve' these issues into a true 'verdict'? The tribunes shamelessly arrogate to themselves the power of formulas such as 'It is decreed'. Sicinius uses a 'shall' that rouses Martius to fury and makes Cominius remark, ''Twas from the canon' (III.i. 89). This is more likely to mean "contrary to established rule', than 'in accordance with it'.[22] But what is 'the canon'? Where is the law by which these people might abide? The whole constitution of Rome is infirm, unresolved and unstable, so that characters on either side keep appealing to rights and obligations that seem to have no foundation in civil law or institutions. There is little if any explicit support in the play itself for the idea of a constitution based on the principle of divided authority—an idea that could act as a real alternative to Martius's impassioned vision of a single authority. None of the other patricians give positive expression to such an idea; they seem to tolerate the institution of the tribunate, but their liberalism, if that is the right word for it, is scarcely enthusiastic. The tribunes are of course themselves prompt to defend their constitutional rights, but they are such low, sneaking fellows that it is difficult to take the rights for which they stand as seriously as one might wish to.

But suppose one stands back from the play itself and from close engagement with its personalities to consider the variety of views open to Shakespeare and his immediate audience around the time of the play's writing. Clifford Chalmers Huffman provides some valuable evidence for the range of theories and attitudes towards republican Rome available during Shakespeare's writing career, and in particular around the early years of James I's reign. Huffman shows how contemporary debate about the theory and practice of government sought for support in the precedents offered by the history of the Roman Republic and Empire, not least in the critical transitions that saw the expulsion of the tyrants at the birth of the Republic and the death of Julius Caesar at its demise. He surveys a range of plays (by Heywood, Lodge, Chapman, Jonson and Shakespeare) that represent subjects from Roman history, to suggest the ways in which these plays necessarily drew on such debates and contributed to them. He argues for the existence within these debates of a body of opinion sympathetic to the whole idea of 'mixed government' as represented by republican Rome (and contemporary Venice), and sympathetic to this not as a remote ideal but as an interpretation of the actual practice of English government itself. With the change of monarch, James's absolutist pretensions put severe pressure on this belief in the intrinsic division and balance of power in the English constitution. In the clashes between James and Parliament the terms of dispute reveal the vigorous currency of the models provided by Roman history, above all in the image of the tribunate, the crucial institution through which the voice of 'the people' could be heard. Huffman shows James's readiness to identify his

Parliamentary antagonists as 'the tribunes of the people', citing his reference in the Parliamentary session convened in November 1606 to 'tribunes of the people whose mouths could not be stopped'.[23]

Huffman helpfully establishes the vigorous and dangerous climate of debate into which Shakespeare's *Coriolanus* would necessarily have entered around this time. But he proceeds to a grimly sceptical reading of the play itself as necessarily endorsing James's own authoritarian position. (Geoffrey Hill's essay on *Cymbeline* offers a helpfully subtle account of the difficulties encountered by Shakespeare in serving this particular, or indeed any worldly patron.)[24] The key factor in Huffman's interpretation is Shakespeare's representation of the tribunes, to whom he applies words from James's own *Basilikon Doron*:

> evil leaders—really misleaders—of the people, dramatic parallels of King James's Puritan antagonists who sought 'to become *Tribuni plebis*: and so in a populare government by leading the people by the nose, to beare the sway of all the rule.'[25]

But one could just as easily take the play to be critical of James's role in creating an absolutist climate which polarised factions intó extremes. If challenged, Shakespeare could indeed claim to have chosen a presentation of the tribunes 'consonant' with James's view of his antagonists, without actually endorsing it. In fact there is an understandable blur in Huffman's argument. He primarily suggests that the play acquiesces in a political stance congenial to James's ruling ideology, by providing ammunition for the disparagement of the model of mixed government represented by republican Rome. But at the same time he proposes that the play positively represents the hardening of political positions in the incipient extremism of the early seventeenth century. Thus the play can be read as critical of *all* the parties involved.

The play 'speaks extremities', to adapt Volumnia's words ('But when extremities speak', III.ii. 41). What measures can possibly avert the confusion that threatens to cleave the city in twain? Volumnia provides a possible answer in the next scene. She has been absent from the stage since her son's triumphal return to Rome (II.i). Now, when she enters to face him we sense that she alone, if anyone, will be able to bend this intransigent man to the part that he must play.

There is an acrid comedy in her efforts to rehearse Martius in a part which it stretches credulity to believe him capable of playing. It certainly stretches his own credulity, and there is a suggestion that it stretches Volumnia's. The sheer force of the images with which he anticipates the culmination of disaster makes us feel that it would need an equal force to stop him in his tracks (III.ii. 1–6). So far from flinching from the prospect of being hurled off the Tarpeian Rock, he glories in the sheer idea of 'precipitation'. The word gives substance to a quality of his being as much as it promises a literal fate to be suffered by his body. Martius thinks of himself as all or nothing.

Volumnia tries belatedly to school her son in the uses of the paradox that a man may play a part which is all *and* nothing. The belatedness is both comical and horrifying. To play such a part is to engage in a shared, collective fiction, a seeming. But to ask him now to play such a part runs utterly athwart all the lessons that she has previously taught him. The 'thwartings' of his 'dispositions' (III.ii. 21) are as nothing compared to what she asks of him now. She has taught him to ignore with contempt the audience that he must now appeal to with 'policy'. The analogy she draws between war and peace is a monstrous fiction. We can just believe that Martius may have said that 'Honour and policy ... I'th'war do grow together' (III.ii. 42–3), but it is difficult to imagine the Martius we know choosing to take in a town with gentle words as a prudent alternative to bloodshed (III.ii. 59–61). When has Martius ever measured the expense of blood, his own and others'? More importantly, the analogy she suggests between the roles of policy in war and in peace implies that the real relationship between Martius and the Roman people is one of war, and that once Martius has 'taken them in', he will treat them as he would treat a vanquished enemy. If this is the case, then the tribunes are quite justified in mobilising the people's fears. This strengthens our sense that there is something more honourable than any of the other patricians can understand, least of all Volumnia, in Martius's inability to stomach the deception that such 'policy' entails. If this is what policy means, he wants no part of it.

Volumnia has been the source for the words which are rooted most deeply in him: words such as 'noble' and 'absolute'. The word 'mild' is not in his vocabulary. She has schooled him in the perfect separation of the various spheres of life; male and female, friends and enemies, patricians and plebeians, hardness and softness, blood and tears. Mildness, softness, tenderness—these are qualities to be disparaged and contemned: 'female' qualities which the women of Rome, at least under Volumnia's tutelage, will have done their best to abjure. Virgilia is an exception in her resistance to this tutelage, and Martius seems to make an exception for her, in his tenderness towards her tenderness. But she makes no visible impression on his general acceptance of his mother's derogation of softness. Except in a wife in whose loyalty he puts an absolute trust, such qualities are treacherous.

Volumnia suggests the insidious tenacity of her lifelong teaching, when she uses image of 'the ripest mulberry/That will not hold the handling' (III.ii. 79–80), to characterise the false humility of heart that Martius must show his audience. It is not just a ripe mulberry but an overripe one: the very excess of the image conveys the contempt which she feels for the sentiment it is supposed to represent, and for the hearers who will be taken in by such theatrical devices. Both mother and son associate softness of any kind with degeneration:

once to be soft is to be instantly and entirely 'rotten'.
'Rotten' is a powerful word in Martius's vocabulary, the
antonym of firmness, constancy, certainty. In the very act of
appealing to her son to counterfeit a mildness, Volumnia
unwittingly excites in him all that fear and loathing of being
'soft', which she has so rigorously inculcated.

Can the words which the tongue utters be merely 'roted'
in it, or do they inevitably take root (III.ii. 55–6)? The Folio
has Volumnia advise her son to use 'such words/That are
but roated in your Tongue'. Modern editors follow Malone
in printing this as 'rote', but Johnson's emendation to 'root',
though less plausible, points to a hesitation which may be
heard in the word.[26] This doubt is at the root of Martius's
hesitation in this scene, and the source of his most
admirable utterance:

> I will not do't,
> Lest I surcease to honour mine own truth,
> And by my body's action teach my mind
> A most inherent baseness.
>
> (III.ii. 120–3)

How can something that is 'inherent' be taught? The root of
the word is to do with 'sticking', and Martius is afraid that
the baseness will literally stick in him. (It is Shakespeare's
only use of 'inherent':) He is troubled by a doubt as to how
far his self and his qualities *are* rooted and grounded in him.
Volumnia tries now to persuade him that what you merely
say and do by 'rote' need not in any way affect the roots of
your being. Her son is not convinced. Behaviour and being
are for him inseparable. His mother has taught him to
honour as an inviolable possession 'mine own truth'. But he
has also learnt to honour *her* as the sole source of his being.
In the contradiction with which she now faces him, between
his obligations to his own truth and to her, it is not the
prospect of the city cleaving in twain that we glimpse, but
rather of Martius's sense of himself.

The comedy in the scene provides us with a welcome respite from the tumultuous violence of the two public confrontations that it separates. But there is little question which kind of scene is more painful for Martius. His mother's efforts at instant re-education are bewildering, absurd, embarrassing. A good performance—and this scene must be one of the touchstones—should probably make an audience hesitate between the desire to laugh with him and at him. Kitchin describes a delightfully abrupt transition in Olivier's performance, between his two 'what thens?'. (The play is quite rich in such repetitions—Volumnia's 'Yes, yes, yes' and 'Come, come, come'—little gifts for an actor).

> He lent the first 'What then?' his celebrated full brass on a rising inflection, caught Volumnia's eye, paused, deflated and repeated 'what then?' quietly and deferentially. Now he was prepared to listen, as comic, contemptuous *obbligato* to Evans's advice.[27]

Kitchin also preserves the extraordinary effect that Olivier created with the repetition of the word 'mildly':

> For the third time he is supposed to repeat the word 'mildly', which sums up the advice he has been given as to his conduct in face of the plebeians. On this most reluctant of exits Olivier neither spoke the word nor cut it. Instead, at the moment of shaping it with lips and facial muscles, he convulsively retched.[28]

Theatre critics frequently admire this little passage, and there is certainly a lot of scope for the actor to cut a fine figure. In his recording of the role, Richard Burton storms off with a ferocious snarl on the word so absurdly at odds with his temper.[29] One can imagine a drier delivery, with Martius almost enjoying the joke with himself, mocking the outlandish new word, ironically 'roting' it in his tongue as his mother advised him.

There is an awful predictability about the culminating showdown in the market-place. Throughout the first part of the play, we have watched the two major forces in the city being 'wrenched up'. But the authorities deputed to concert the voice of the people have done their job much more efficiently than the patricians who have tried to prompt Martius. The desperate dress rehearsal of the previous scene will collapse with ignominious speed as Martius reverts to the 'disposition' by which he knows himself and is known by others. Menenius and Cominius thrust themselves despairingly into the breach between the parties. Cominius seems to know that the distinction between the citizen and the soldier, to which Menenius appeals, is now beside the point. In a vain and touching last effort, he substitutes himself as an authoritative embodiment of the loyal soldier *and* citizen that he knows the plebeians cannot recognise in Martius himself (III.iii. 109–16).

The tribunes have orchestrated the semblance of a legal process. Yet when Sicinius pronounces the verdict and names the judgment of banishment, there is almost a sense of anti-climax. In the bustling introduction to the scene, he mentioned three possibilities: 'For death, for fine, or banishment' (III.iii. 15). Indeed he goes on to stress the possibilities of 'fine' and 'death', so that when it comes down to it, the choice of banishment is bound to come as a surprising compromise between the lenity and severity of the other two. This slight sense of anti-climax in the tribunes' decision is masked by the noisy unanimity with which the crowd greet the verdict: 'It shall be so, it shall be so!' But it helps to prepare the way for Martius's magnificent final riposte. The delay in his response to Sicinius's formal pronouncement is just sufficient for our expectations to be heightened. What does Martius do, while he listens to Sicinius and the crowd, and Cominius (III.iii. 93–119)? His silence is not so prolonged that we imagine him lost for words, but it is just sufficiently protracted for us to be anxiously conscious that he must have something to say.

One can imagine him stonily immobile in the midst of the
tumult, the rapturous and mindless exultation of the cries:
'It shall be so, it shall be so!' When he does speak, his words
rise unforgettably above the 'din confus'd' that the tribunes
have roused.

There are two obvious theatrical opportunities in the
staging of this speech. The first is to have Martius
outvoicing the tumult by the sheer power of his lungs, his
opening words soaring above it with operatic bravura. The
other is to leave a perceptible pause after his no less bravura
exit line, before the tumult starts up again. In Peter Hall's
1984–5 National Theatre production, Ian McKellen exited
before delivering Martius's wonderful line 'There is a world
elsewhere' from off-stage, as a magnificent afterthought.
There are other less obvious possibilities, such as to have
the crowd's tumult subside into nervous expectancy even
before Martius begins to speak, cowed by the sheer force of
his ominous silence. In Burton's recording of the title role
the crowd's shouts come to an eerily abrupt halt, before he
begins 'You common cry of curs!'

In his description of Olivier's performance Kitchin
imaginatively recreates the shattering effect of this moment.

> Just before this speech Olivier leaned against the masonry
> high up on Aronson's set, head rolling from side to side,
> eyes mad as those of a Sistine Chapel prophetess while he
> listened to the tribunes. The head movement, I was
> amused to notice, was one recommended by Elsie
> Fogerty to her students for relaxing tension in the neck;
> Olivier was preparing himself. . . . Here, cursing the
> plebeians, he gave the phrases such a charge of emotion
> that he gathered them into a single rhetorical missile, so
> that the speech had an impact like jagged stones parcelled
> together and hurled in somebody's face. There was a
> bizarre impression of one man lynching a crowd.[30]

There is indeed something trembling on the edge of madness

in Martius's magnificent repudiation of reality.

But however it is done or imagined, the effect of this speech must surely be stunning—as stunning as the physical impact of Martius in battle. Martius has recovered himself, and the sense of this is exhilarating. He is free of the rituals and forms, the hypocrisies under which he has been forced to squirm from the moment at which his single combat with Aufidius was interrupted:

> You common cry of curs! whose breath I hate
> As reek o'th'rotten fens, whose loves I prize
> As the dead carcasses of unburied men
> That do corrupt my air: I banish you!
> And here remain with your uncertainty!
> Let every feeble rumour shake your hearts!
> Your enemies, with nodding of their plumes,
> Fan you into despair! Have the power still
> To banish your defenders, till at length
> Your ignorance—which finds not till it feels,
> Making but reservation of yourselves,
> Still your own foes—deliver you as most
> Abated captives to some nation
> That won you without blows! Despising
> For you the city, thus I turn my back.
> There is a world elsewhere!
>
> (III.iii. 120–35)

The withering contempt that he feels for his audience powers him over the curbs and embarquements of the syntax. There are the magnificent gestural certainties of 'I banish you', and 'thus I turn my back'. There is the deliciously contemptuous laughter in the image of the enemies who will 'with nodding of their plumes/Fan you into despair'. Scarcely anything in the play gives such a peculiar twist to our sense of his humour as the delightfully serene dismissiveness in his choice of the word 'fan'. This effect will be repeated near the end of the play when he alights so choicely on the word 'flutter'—'I/Flutter'd your Volscians in Corioles' (V.vi. 114–15).

The rapturous certainty of the speech is so stunning that as we hear the words 'There is a world elsewhere', it is difficult to take in what they mean. In the theatre it should be impossible to find the instant presence of mind to ask: 'where, exactly'? Yet, as is the way with this play, the words linger to gather resonance. They will certainly hang in the air and cling in the mind throughout the subsequent phases of the play—and after it has ended.

·4·

'O world, thy slippery turns!'

The huge first movement of the play culminates in Martius's banishment from Rome. There have been movements within this large trajectory: from the opening scene in Rome, out to the battlefield and back to Rome, then from triumph to catastrophe. It is difficult to disagree with Emrys Jones's conclusion that the Folio division which marks the beginning of Act 4 obscures the decisive line of demarcation after what modern editions call Act 4 Scene 2.[1]

Catastrophe is what it seems to Martius's friends and family. They represent an impressively collective grief, as uncalculatedly concerted as the joy at his triumphal entry. Yet now as then, Martius stands apart from the show of collective feeling. He is still under the heady influence of the previous scene and he seems to feel a relief at having extricated himself from an intolerable situation. It is left to Volumnia and Cominius gingerly to imagine what kind of future can lie ahead of him, as he faces a 'wild exposure' (IV.i. 36), 'a single man' in 'the vast world' (IV.i. 42). Volumnia's image of a wild exposure recalls with painful irony that original exposure to which she submitted his tender body when she sent him out to the cruel wars. But there his course lay clear ahead of him. Now she comes as near to expressing a desire to protect him as she has ever done. It is a thought to which she is a stranger, as the Camillo

who offers such a promptly protective response to the plight
of the young lovers in *The Winter's Tale* is not. He knows
from experience the perils ahead of 'a wild dedication of
yourselves/To unpath'd waters, undream'd shores, most
certain/To miseries enough' (*The Winter's Tale*, IV.iv.
558–60).

But why should Martius need protection? There may
even be a tinge of irritation in his feelings towards the 'sad
women' whose grief might imply that he is not capable of
looking after himself, as he has always done in the past.
Astonishing as it may be, he does not seem to feel that
anything significant has changed. *He* has not changed. Have
not all the lessons which he has learnt from his mother and
from the wars—and which he now quotes back at Volumnia
and Cominius with a more or less gentle, bewildered,
impatient remonstrance—schooled him into hardness? It is
impossible to fathom his feelings or his plans at this point.
He is free, that is all, and it is an elation that he recognises.
He has spent his rage on the people of Rome, for the time
being. There is a sprightliness in the ease with which he
shrugs off his mother's rabid invocation of the 'red
pestilence':

> What, what, what!
> I shall be lov'd when I am lack'd.   (IV.i. 14–15)

It is difficult to believe that he feels no pain in the severance
from his family, his friends and his city, but this kind of pain
is what he is used to. He is used to leaving his city and his
loved ones. The pain of such departures is swallowed up by
the pleasure of anticipation at being and doing out there,
beyond the city walls. Out there, in the hostile world
elsewhere, in the face of 'the enemy', he is in his element. Is
it any different this time?

That he must know, or at least be holding at bay the
knowledge that it *will* be different, is suggested by the lines in
which he compares himself to

> a lonely dragon that his fen
> Makes fear'd and talk'd of more than seen.
>
> (IV.i. 30–1)

We cannot know how seriously he takes this image of himself, or how far it may be prompted by a desire to impress his listeners rather than, or as well as, himself. He certainly does not want company and is firm but polite in his rejection of Cominius's offer. It is a surprising fact that while 'alone' is a common word in Shakespeare, the *OED* registers this as the first recorded use of the word 'lonely' in the English language. It is as if Shakespeare were making Martius find a new syllable, to 'exceed the common' (IV.i. 32). One may even hear in his voice a humorous delight in the chill he knows that he can inspire in other people. These wretched Romans insist on such fearful talk about him, behind his back and to his face. This has irritated him, both lightly and grossly. But if that is what they want, he will enjoy the thought of really giving them something to talk about, around which to monger their fearful fantasies. Perhaps this will solace his mother too.

His mother certainly needs some solace, and so does his wife. They find a little relief in their confrontation with the tribunes. The tribunes are already consolidating their political gains. They will humble themselves now, as Martius so fatally failed to. Already we begin to recognise the reformation of a status quo, in which the personal anger and grief of Volumnia and Virgilia will be impotent to dislodge the new grip which the tribunes hold over the day-to-day affairs of the city. The women can 'unclog' their hearts for a moment or two, but nothing they can say will make any difference. It is not pleasant to have someone calling the 'hoarded plague o'th'gods' down on your head (IV.ii. II), but one can find something to admire, against the grain, in the tribunes' coolness. This sort of contumacious skirmish has the ring of daily life to it, a chance but common occurrence in the Rome from which Martius has been banished. In its way this scene balances the encounter between Menenius and the tribunes that just preceded Martius's triumphal re-entry into Rome. Both give a flavour of the daily, habitual acrimony that simmers along the streets of Rome.

Volumnia said of her son that 'before him he carries noise, and behind him he leaves tears' (II.i. 157–8). Amongst the Volsces he left behind him not only the tears of widows but also the anger of Aufidius. In Rome he has left behind him both tears and anger. With a massive and awesome summoning of will, Volumnia rises to the utterance of an image that will resound after her, the image of a coldly remorseless anger, at once self-devouring and self-nourishing. Menenius had innocently invited her to sup with him. He could be forgiven for being taken aback by her response:

> Anger's my meat: I sup upon myself
> And so shall starve with feeding. Come, let's go.
> Leave this faint puling, and lament as I do,
> In anger, Juno-like. Come, come, come!
>
> (IV.ii. 50–3)

This is more impressive than any of the curses which she levels at the tribunes. It harbours an obscure threat, as if Volumnia were dedicating herself to a kind of death, or living death. Her words seem to draw perversely on an image of sacrifice, such as the famous emblem of maternal selflessness, the pelican mother who nourishes her young with her own flesh. What sort of food has Volumnia ever given to her own child? She has taught him not to need food, and to despise the need of others for food. Now she is fulfilling the logic of her whole ethos in the sheer assertion of a perfect self-sufficiency, the willed withdrawal of resources from the normal rhythms of physical necessity. This image of godlike anger corresponds to Martius's image of the lonely dragon in its fen. Both mother and son leave us

with resounding, ominous images of self-withdrawal, a
harbouring of measureless resources, godlike and bestial.
Granville-Barker comments eloquently on these lines:
'These are the natures—like mother, like son—to be
broken, never bent; born to catastrophe'.[2] Yet when mother
and son next meet, it will not be a meeting between a god and
a beast, between Juno and the dragon, but—at least as
Martius imagines it—the less equal meeting of Olympus and
(oh, strange transformation for a dragon and his fen) a
molehill.

The next phase of the play poses some of the most difficult
and interesting problems for the interpretation of Martius's
character and of the play as a whole. Here is a man whose
identity has been powerfully moulded by the expectations
which other people have of him—his family, his friends and
colleagues and enemies, his 'society'. Now for the first time
he has been cut loose from that life, violently and
absolutely. And so far from repining at the loss of job and
status and the paraphernalia of that old world, he has
himself been an active accomplice in the process—he has
helped to cut himself loose: 'I banish you'.

All Shakespearian tragic characters are more or less
violently dislodged from an old self and world that have
known each other, by which they have known themselves
and been known by others. Romeo and Juliet, Brutus,
Hamlet, Othello, Lear, Timon, Macbeth—they are all made
strange to themselves by the invasion of a future for which
they were unprepared but in which they have in some way
colluded. The shock of this invasion lays bare the prospect
of doing and thinking and feeling to which the old self in the
old world could never have found access. The self and the
world are not after all given entities, finished, final,
complete; they are still to be made and discovered. This
discovery is in various measures exhilarating and terrifying,
not only for those immediately involved in such experiences
but also for the audience looking on at the world of the play.
There is terror at the danger that nothing will survive the

fearful passage from the old self and world into the new. There is exhilaration at the thought that anything which can survive the rigour of such a passage will have proved its worth indeed.

In all these tragic characters there is something precipitate that spurs them onwards to take the plunge or make the break, some lack of restraint or prudence or fear. In some lights Martius can seem close to a parody of such a tragic figure. He seems not to know the meaning of restraint or prudence or fear. Compared with other Shakespearian tragic figures, he positively hurls himself towards the break with the world he has known. He does not hesitate or reflect or imagine the consequences. If Rome refuses to meet his idea of a state and refuses to accept him as he is, then good riddance to it:

> Despising
> For you the city, thus I turn my back.
>
> (III.iii. 133–4)

He lives as if he had nothing to lose. It is as if he has become immune to the sense of risk, or never known it. His mother says that she was 'pleased to let him seek danger' (I.iii. 12–13), and danger has so pleased him that it has left little room for anything else. Physical danger is his element, and in the great climactic confrontation with the Roman populace he is in it. When he bids farewell to Rome, the grief and the sense of loss is all embodied in his family and friends. But there may be kinds of danger of which he has no inkling as yet, kinds of danger which cannot be outfaced by brute force, in word or deed.

What troubles and excites readers and spectators at this point is the uncertainty as to how this man will grasp the opportunity with which he is faced. Some critics express disappointment with Shakespeare's failure to endow him with a deepening consciousness of the new world into which he has broken when he passes out of Rome. There is no heath outside the city walls, no witches and no poor Toms. There is no Dover cliff, no sea, not even after all a fen in which he could fancy himself as a dragon. There is no wilderness, no empty or 'wild' space in which he could face the strangeness in himself and give it utterance, as Lear and Macbeth do. Or to put it the other way round, Martius does not have it in him—the power to bring such a memorable alien space into being. He does not deserve the great imaginative landscapes of Lear and Macbeth, so he does not find one.[3]

But this play is quite different in method from *Lear* and *Macbeth* (which are different enough from each other). Its revelations are much more oblique, surreptitious, fugitive. Because its central figure does not express himself as generously and variously as other tragic characters, we need not conclude that he has nothing to express. It is exactly the urge to reach conclusions that the play so remorselessly teases. The fact that we see so many of the characters falling prey to this urge should alert us to resist it.

We do not see Martius in a wilderness between Rome and Antium. Instead we glimpse a chance encounter between two secret agents that turns on the question of names. The Roman secret agent says that he *knows* the man he meets on the road, and *thinks* his name is Adrian. In fact he goes slightly further than this in saying not only 'I know you well sir' but also 'and you know me'. The Roman cannot quite say that they know *each other* until the Volscian confirms the little pact. This is where names and thinking come in. Names help people to recognise each other, and they recognise each other or admit to their knowing each other—by thinking. By thinking what, exactly? Soon Martius will find a construction that puts the matter as nicely as one could wish, when he says that for Aufidius to recognise him, Aufidius will have to think him for the man he is: other people think us.

Our first sight of Martius since he left Rome finds him standing in front of Aufidius's house. But a theatre audience will not instantly recognise him, 'in mean apparel, disguised and muffled'. His appearance should be a shock to us. It may well be 'a potent visual suggestion that something in the man himself, not just in his circumstances, has changed'.[4] Like the other Roman traitor, Nicanor, it will be his 'tongue' by which the audience recognise him.

Martius announces himself to the audience by apostrophising the city whose widows he has made, a city which he admires as 'goodly' even as he recognises how utterly beyond the bounds of its possible hospitality his past actions have put him. He tells us of his intention to seek out Aufidius. We are left thus poised in expectation, as he is left alone on stage and begins to speak. Why has he come here?

> O world, thy slippery turns! Friends now fast sworn,
> Whose double bosoms seems to wear one heart,
> Whose hours, whose bed, whose meal and exercise
> Are still together, who twin, as 'twere, in love
> Unseparable, shall within this hour,
> On a dissension of a doit, break out
> To bitterest enmity: so fellest foes,
> Whose passions and whose plots have broke their
>   sleep
> To take the one the other, by some chance,
> Some trick not worth an egg, shall grow dear friends
> And interjoin their issues. So with me:
> My birthplace hate I, and my love's upon
> This enemy town. I'll enter: if he slay me
> He does fair justice; if he give me way,
> I'll do his country service.
>
>   (IV.iv. 12–26)

This speech may make us feel that Martius does not himself know what he is doing, and that he is here trying to find an explanation. He is making generalisations about the role which chance plays in even the most seemingly durable relations, of enmity and friendship. It is as if he is trying to persuade himself that all human allegiances, from the most trivial to the most profound, are governed by the same principle of chance that we have just seen at work in the meeting between the two secret agents. There is an astonishing gracelessness in the lines in which he applies these generalisations to himself: 'My birthplace hate I, and my love's upon/This enemy town'. The sheer numbness of this suggests that his thoughts are not really on Rome and Antium at all: they are on Aufidius, the nameless 'he' of his next words. He is not trying to understand his rejection of and by Rome, or to plot his future revenge on it. He is only interested in Aufidius, in the pure hazard of meeting the man in the world who hates him most.

It is only later, in the scene with Aufidius, that he speaks of his desire for revenge. When he does so, it becomes possible to read backwards and forwards a consistent grip on this motive. But the burden of imputing this consistent intention is thrown on to us, as readers or spectators. It is quite different in Plutarch, who patiently explains that from the moment that his banishment is pronounced he is dominated by 'the vehemencie of anger, and desire of revenge'.[5] His seemingly irrational action in seeking out Aufidius is thus given an entirely rational explanation, one which Martius himself would have no hesitation in accepting: 'In the ende, seeing he could revolve no waye, to take a profitable or hónorable course, but only was pricked forward still to be revenged of the Romaines: he thought to raise up some great warres against them, by their neerest neighbours'.[6] It is conceivable that Shakespeare's Martius has engaged in this sort of deliberation, but we are not made privy to it. This makes us feel that he is himself unclear about his own motives, and that anger and revenge do not exhaust their range. His speech before Aufidius's house concludes with an oddly weighty emphasis on the words 'justice' and 'service'.

In the first part of the play there was only a single scene which firmly established a private, interior space—the scene

with Volumnia, Virgilia and Valeria (I.iii). Virgilia there
said that she would not cross the threshold until her
husband returned from the wars. There is only one other
scene in the play which distinctly establishes a comparable
inner space. It is the scene in which Martius crosses
Aufidius's threshold and is welcomed to his hearth. The
word threshold occurs only twice in the play (and only six
times in all anywhere in Shakespeare), first when Virgilia
vows that she will not leave her domestic space and,
secondly, when Aufidius recalls his wife entering his own. In
fact Aufidius chooses a strikingly masterful word to
describe his wife's entrance when he says that he saw her
'bestride' his threshold. The young Martius achieved one of
his first great feats in battle when 'he bestrid/An o'erpress'd
Roman' (II.ii. 92–3). Aufidius is using a construction typical
of the play, when he makes a disparaging comparison
between his wife's passage across his threshold and
Martius's:

> more dances my rapt heart
> Than when I first my wedded mistress saw
> Bestride my threshold.
>
> (IV.v. 117–19)

It is surely Martius who makes him feel that his threshold is
being 'bestrid', but by transference he ascribes this mastery
to his wife.

Martius has shown an awesome ability to carve his
passage through the barriers that can be manned and broken
by brute force. He has no patience with any other kind of
barriers, mere walls of words. We have seen him for
ourselves threading the gates of Corioles, triumphally
entering the gates of Rome, even managing to exit from
those same gates with more than enough dignity to dispel
the smirch of humiliation. Soon we will hear from one of
Aufidius's servants of his vow to 'sowl the porter of Rome
gates by th'ears', and that he will 'mow all down before him,

and leave his passage polled' (IV.v. 206–8). The general view of him in the play, to which even the tribunes are not immune, is that 'Coriolanus' is the name for an irresistible force, whose course will on the way it takes, bearing down all before it.

All this lends by contrast the scene at Aufidius's threshold a peculiar distinction. Even before Aufidius's entrance we recognise something eerily unfamiliar about Martius's manner. Usually he knows where he is going and just marches straight in. How odd, from his mouth, sound the courtesies with which he asks the passing citizen directions to Aufidius's house ('if it be your will', 'beseech you', 'thank you'). For most people this would simply be normal politeness, but for Martius this is shockingly good behaviour. Can it be that he actually feels more at home in this 'goodly city', in front of this 'goodly house', where 'the feast smells well', than he ever did in Rome? Or that he would like to? Even in the acrimonious exchanges with Aufidius's servants there is something unfamiliar in the grotesquely ribald tone he adopts: ''tis an honester service than to meddle with thy mistress' (IV.v. 48–9). He is not used to passing the time of day with his social inferiors, and he has only descended to this jocular repartee on another occasion when he was not himself—the scene in which he stood 'disguised' in the Roman market-place.

Aufidius's house is very different from the domestic interior in which Martius's women-folk waited for him. It is a bustling, festive household, a social centre such as we never glimpse in Rome. It is difficult to imagine Martius ever holding a feast in *his* house to entertain the lords of Rome. Menenius alone upholds a style of good cheer for which the Rome that we see for ourselves allows little opportunity. But in Antium festivity such as we hear in the background seems to be more the order of the day. The feast is Shakespeare's creation: in Plutarch, Aufidius simply happens to be 'at supper', without any of the other Volscian lords.[7] Here music plays, the wine flows, there is a *hearth* to the house. Shakespeare finds the word 'harthe' in North, but it carries a slight stress in this scene. Martius says to the servants, with teasing alliteration, that he 'will not hurt your hearth' (IV.v. 26). He tells Aufidius that 'this extremity/ Hath brought me to thy hearth. . . ' (IV.v. 79–80). Aufidius's 'hearth' sounds close to the 'heart' to which both Martius and Aufidius himself shortly make several pointed references: 'Then if thou hast/A heart of wreak in thee. . .' (IV.v. 85–6); 'Each word thou hast spoke hath weeded from my heart. . . ' (IV.v. 103); 'more dances my rapt heart. . .' (IV.v. 117). Near the end of the play, as Aufidius obsessively rehearses the history of Martius's treachery, the word turns out to have stuck in his gullet: 'being banish'd for't, he came unto my hearth' (V.vi. 30). It is surprising to find that apart from one other occurrence in the plural, this is the only play in which Shakespeare avails himself of the word. Aufidius is the only character in Shakespeare to have a hearth.

There is a suppressed comedy in the passage in which Martius and Aufidius come face to face. Shakespeare seizes on the hint of a hesitation in Plutarch's account of the critical moment and proceeds to embarrass the formalities.

> Then Martius unmuffled him selfe, and after he had paused a while, making no aunswer, he sayed unto him: 'If thou knowest me not yet, Tullus, and seeing me, doest not perhappes beléeve me to be the man I am in dede, I must of necessitie bewraye my self to be that I am. I am *Caius Martius*.'[8]

Plutarch has stressed the power invested in Martius's deliberate disguise. Shakespeare retains this sense of the stranger's power, but he also brings out the paradoxical pathos of his anonymity by prolonging the momentary silence or 'pause', as Martius waits to be recognised for the man he is in deed.

This has the effect of arousing some solemn echoes of ritual, of the transition rites preceding an act of 'incorporation' or 'adoption'. Arnold van Gennep comments on the paradoxical status of the alien stranger awaiting admission:

> such a person is weak, because he is outside a given group or society, but he is also strong, since he is in the sacred realm with respect to the group's members, for whom their society constitutes the secular world. In consequence, some peoples kill, strip, and mistreat a stranger without ceremony, while others fear him, take great care of him, treat him as a powerful being, or take magico-religious protective measures against him.[9]

This may help to explain Martius's ghoulish reference to 'the city of kites and crows': it is a faint attempt to play the ritual role set down for him, as the mysterious stranger from the realm of the sacred. It is difficult to know whether he takes it any more seriously than all the other formalities in which he finds himself embroiled. He is likely to be playing on the servants' superstitions. Much more serious is the question of how Aufidius will face up to his role. How happily will *he* fulfil his responsibilities as the host who receives the weak/strong stranger? Van Gennep's comments suggest the ominously powerful impulse towards one of two extremes, either towards the murderous degradation of the stranger or towards his deification. It may be worth remembering this as we watch Martius's career amid his new host-group, and as we consider the pulling power of the many ritual forms throughout the play.

Martius must surrender his name to gain admission. Later on Menenius faces a barrier at which he finds that the virtue of his name is 'not here passable' (V.ii. 12). As we attend with apprehension to the meeting of Martius and Aufidius, we are bound to wonder what kind of credit Martius's name will find: what *is* his name? Aufidius has vowed that next time he meets Martius, he will get him, no matter what. This is the next time.

But Aufidius does not recognise him, and Shakespeare chooses to highlight this awkwardness. In *Henry VI, Part I*, there is a delightful moment at which the Countess of Auvergne first lays eyes on the English hero Lord Talbot. She cannot believe that after all that she has heard about the mighty warrior, this is the man in front of her:

> Alas, this is a child, a silly dwarf!
> It cannot be this weak and writhled shrimp
> Should strike such terror to his enemies.
>   (*Henry VI, Part I*, II.iii. 22–4)

Talbot soon has the last laugh, unfortunately. There are no women (or any other dissidents) in *Coriolanus* to cast such direct derision on the pretensions of the warrior males, and one thing for sure is that Martius is no 'weak and writhled shrimp'. Nevertheless, there *is* something underhandedly risible in the fact that Aufidius, of all people, should not know Martius when he sees him. He had no difficulty on the battlefield. Before he knows him he has to 'think him for the man he is', as Martius so pregnantly puts it. Aufidius has to ask him his name no less than six times before at last Martius names himself. By the time he eventually does so, the sheer protractedness of the little ceremony makes it seem like a kind of defeat, that Martius has to put himself into words before Aufidius can recognise him.

Throughout this nervy passage of dialogue, and even more so as he listens to the long speech into which Martius then launches, there is scope to wonder what is going on in Aufidius—and scope, of course, for an actor. It is possible to imagine and play his requests for Martius's name with a simply rising impatience, or a more nonchalant curiosity, either of which can be frozen into immobility at the eventual moment of revelation: 'My name is Caius Martius'. But it is possible to imagine his curiosity growing to the point at which the truth may half-dawn on him before the revelation itself. It is even possible to suppose that the truth *does* dawn just before his final denial and request, so that they become an outright challenge: 'I know thee not. Thy name?' This would certainly have the effect of tilting the battle of wills decisively, if momentarily, in Aufidius's favour. Plutarch gives Aufidius no immediate reaction to the news. Narrative does not need to concern itself with the reactions of listeners. But as soon as it is dramatised, Aufidius's silent audition to Martius's long speech becomes fraught with interest. It is a long listening.

How *is* Aufidius going to react when Martius's speech comes to an end? Again the contrast with the narrative source is instructive. There his reaction is entirely unproblematic, and he makes a graciously brief speech of welcome. Dramatisation instantly creates a new range of possibilities in the gap that separates the end of Martius's speech and the beginning of Aufidius's. The actor can choose to minimise this gap—or to pause, however fractionally, before saying, 'O Martius, Martius!' In the second and climactic confrontation in the latter part of the play, Martius breaks the long silence in which he has listened to his mother's supplication with a similarly tolling repetition, 'O mother, mother!' In both cases the listener has been faced with an 'impossible' choice, and the plaintive, remorseful repetition marks the difficulty, and perhaps impossibility, of giving full vent to the complexity of his feelings. 'O Màrtius, Martius!'—of course Aufidius has no choice but to yield to the suppliant's appeal.

The speech which Shakespeare creates for Aufidius here is one of the masterstrokes of the play. What has happened to the man who earlier vowed implacable revenge? There is an easily recognisable problem in the continuity of Martius's character as it is represented in the play. But this is shadowed by the problem of Aufidius and his character. It is a long time since we last saw him, and as we listen to the fulsome terms in which he now welcomes his sworn enemy, it is impossible to be certain how far his 'ancient malice' has faded or retained its vigour. It is difficult to believe that this

speech of welcome is a calculated exercise in deception. Yet
it is no less difficult to gauge its sincerity. What form could
sincerity possibly take under these circumstances? The same
question is posed by the moment at which Martius later has
to respond to Volumnia's appeal—and more honourably
answered by his response. Aufidius does not know what he
feels here. He is dazzled by Martius's presence. Granville-
Barker points out that he has presumably had a few drinks,
though where the effects of wine end and the effects of
Martius's presence begin it is impossible to tell.[10] Martius is
the stuff his dreams are made on, and now this dream-image,
this 'nothing', is here before him in the flesh, laying his life at
his feet.

What Martius and Aufidius represent for each other is
repetition.[11] There is an uncanny beauty to the lines in
which Aufidius celebrates the repeated shattering and
scattering of his manhood against

> that body, where against
> My grained ash an hundred times hath broke,
> And scarr'd the moon with splinters.
>
> (IV.v. 108–10)

His speech is a series of lunging attempts to steady himself,
to resist the star-struck wonder inspired by the materialising
of this dream-image. As it progresses, he manages to purge it
of the more embarrassing evidence of his rapture ('thou
noble thing', 'thou Mars'). By the time he has finished he has
impulsively and disastrously handed over to Martius a
joint-share in the leading of the Volscian army, without
even consulting the Volscian senators. Fortunately they are
as easily bowled over by Martius as Aufidius himself. But it
is noticeable that in Plutarch both Aufidius and the Volscian
lords behave with far less precipitation. There Aufidius
soberly counsels his colleagues to take Martius into their
service, and they are themselves impressed by Martius's
eloquence.[12]

Martius also has to listen at length to Aufidius. His sole words in response to Aufidius's welcome are, 'You bless me, gods!' (IV.v. 136). There are problems and opportunities here for the actors concerned, who have to listen in silence to each other. The whole style of this scene between the two men is thrown into sharp relief by the garrulous, sociable chatter of the serving-men that follows hot on its heels. It is as if Martius and Aufidius are talking *at* each other rather than to or with each other. Shakespeare may have taken a hint here from North's calling Martius's long speech an 'oration'.

Here it is worth helping to preserve a remarkable reading of this scene and its place in the play as a whole, in Olivier's 1959 performance. Kitchin is celebrating Olivier's general 'interpretative intelligence':

> There was no doubt at all where the play's climax comes. It is on the sealing of their pact, or so I shall always believe after Olivier's extraordinary handshake. He had been very quiet during the scene. There was a deathly, premonitory misgiving in the way he eventually shook hands; and his eyes glazed. Whatever integration the character of Marcius had possessed fell apart at that moment. The rest was crumble, detonation and collapse, with part of him fatalistically detached.[13]

This makes one think of Hazlitt's generously exaggerated claim that 'actors are the best commentators on the poets'.[14] The image of the handshake draws its power from the suspense of the long silence that it breaks. And although Kitchin does not make this point, this handshake gathers further significance from the connection and contrast that it will make with the more famously culminating gesture when Martius holds his *mother's* hand, in silence.[15]

Aufidius's servants provide a valuable perspective on their master and the other Volscian lords. For all the aura of revelry in the house, it is important that the feast takes place

off-stage. There remains something insubstantial to this
feast, to which Martius's own dreamlike apparition adds a
crowning unreality. The servants do not protest at the
reception accorded him but they are capable of providing
the sobering perspective in which it appears for the
grotesque thing that it is—just as the gesture that seems to
the drunken man who executes it a triumph of elegance and
good taste appears to the sober onlooker the antic of a
buffoon: 'Our general himself makes a mistress of him,
sanctifies himself with's hand, and turns up the white
o'th'eye to his discourse' (IV.v. 199–202).

It is only a momentary glimpse, for the servants are
themselves excited and their own mixed feelings tumble
against each other with a pleasant congeniality. It is one of
the most sociable passages in the play. They resolve with an
admirable amicability the problem that Martius poses to
their feelings of loyalty to Aufidius: 'Come, we are fellows
and friends: he was ever too hard for him; I have heard him
say so himself' (IV.v. 187–9). They are quite different in
temper and tone from their Roman counterparts, the men
they have presumably met on the battlefield, and look
forward to meeting again. They owe a personal loyalty to
Aufidius such as we see nothing of in Rome, where the lower
orders are all thoroughly urbanised, skilled or unskilled
labourers owing no loyalty to a master. This may free and
sharpen the Romans' political intelligence, but it also leaves
them riper for manipulation by the mastery of words, both
the patricians' and the tribunes'. In so far as we begin to
form a distinguishable image of the Volscian commoners,
they seem to belong to an older feudal order. Their speech
amongst themselves is companionable and effervescent; it
has the smack of a gratuitous relish such as we do not hear
from the more anxious mouths of the Roman poor.

Yet Antium and Aufidius's hearth are only, all told, the
sketch of a world elsewhere. The conviviality that they offer
has no depth to it. This is partly because, like the domestic
world adamantly guarded by Virgilia, it is given so little time

to develop before our eyes and in our ears. Aufidius himself
plays the role of the gracious host and gathers the wandering
outcast to his hearth. Yet the role is one which is forced on
him. He cannot refuse it, but to accept it will mean living
with consequences which in the 'rapture' of the moment it is
easy to avoid facing. When we next see Aufidius the rapture
will have worn off. He will have sobered up.

If Aufidius's hearth presents an evanescent model of
conviviality, our next view of Rome presents a more sharply
ironic model of the social harmony that Martius has left
behind him in Rome. The tribunes are purring with self-
satisfaction as they taunt Menenius with the good times that
they have ushered in, 'Our tradesmen singing in their shops
and going/About their functions friendly' (IV.vi. 8–9). The
'singing' lends this the unreal sheen of a party political
broadcast, but the little vignette of a street scene in which
the citizens bless their new patrons seems to confirm the
improbably utopian climate that has suddenly bloomed in
Rome. It is a nice little dream while it lasts.

This is the first time in the play that we have seen a Rome
that is free of Martius. All of a sudden, Rome hardly seems a
worthy adversary for Martius. In the first part of the play
there was an elation in the way Martius stood 'alone', on the
battlefield and in the city, against the great tide, the sheer
multitude of his foes. Now all that excitement has been
dispelled by the sheer logic of military power. Martius is no
longer alone, and the destruction of Rome is a foregone
conclusion.

The disappointment is perhaps a calculated one. It serves
to point us towards the different dangers which Martius
now faces. These dangers are no longer to be met head-on in
the thronging tumult of the battlefield and market-place. It
is no longer a matter of slaying and being slain, of vowing
and cursing. The dangers now take the shape of Aufidius
and Volumnia. The switch from the seething, fearful streets
of Rome to the private colloquy between Aufidius and his
lieutenant marks the shifting currents of dramatic energy.

From this point on there will be an increasing divergence of interest between the fate of Rome and the fate of Martius. This juxtaposition will occur again, to chilling effect, when the scene of jubilation at Rome's salvation gives way suddenly to Aufidius's conspiratorial whispers.

The suddenness with which Aufidius has fallen out of love with his new colleague comes as a shock, and it cannot but send our minds back to ponder again the quality of the greeting he accorded him only a few moments ago. What Aufidius has to say about Martius here carries a certain authority to it, if only because he is speaking in private, and to an anonymous auditor whom we have no reason to believe he feels the need to impress. When people have talked about Martius's virtues and vices, as they have done incessantly, we have usually been conscious of their own interests in calling him proud or ambitious, a planet or a viper. We have usually been conscious of a positive need or desire to believe what they say, or to have their auditors believe it. So that there has always been something public about the way people speak of him, even if they have actually been speaking in private, as Volumnia was to Virgilia or the tribunes were to each other. What they have to say sounds rehearsed, whether it is so or not.

This is where Aufidius's speech gathers authority. It does not strike us as premeditated. Aufidius sounds self-forgetful and forgetful of his ostensible auditor, the sympathetic lieutenant. This is a more arduously uncalculated attempt to explain Martius than at any other point in the play. But it does not follow from this that Aufidius is more successful than anyone else. G. R. Hibbard comments that 'Shakespeare takes this opportunity to sum up his hero's character, as it has appeared so far, and to give a number of possible interpretations of his earlier behaviour'.[16] But as with all the images of nature and machinery and divinity attributed to Martius throughout the play, Shakespeare has put this summary into the mouth of a particular character. The summary and the interpretations are significant not so much for what they reveal about Martius as for what they reveal about the impossibility of satisfactorily summing him up.

There is an honourable candour in the confusion of Aufidius's speech—he *wants* to understand. Martius matters to him as intimately as he matters to anyone in the play, including Volumnia and Virgilia. But what we hear is the restless, 'choking' sound of a man rapidly summoning and as rapidly discarding one kind of explanatory model after another, as he tries to understand Martius's past and his future, and what links them together. As far as Martius's victory over Rome is concerned he has no doubts, and the memorable image of Martius's 'natural sovereignty' rolls off his tongue with the ease of resigned admiration:

> I think he'll be to Rome
> As is the osprey to the fish, who takes it
> By sovereignty of nature.
>
> (IV.vii. 33–5)

That presents him with no problem. It is when he tries to understand the inner truth of Martius's history that his language falters. One by one he invokes the moral explanation of 'pride', the political explanation of 'defect of judgment', and the psychological explanation of 'nature'. But his own syntax becomes increasingly 'choked' as he struggles to express the idea of an intrinsic, unravellable relation between Martius's virtues and vices.[17] It is hard to see how much he really succeeds in expressing. The idea that 'our virtues/Lie in th'interpretation of the time' is seized on by some readers as a valuable truth, but it is commonplace enough. It is noticeable that after the most effortful of all his sentences, Aufidius relapses at last into proverbial simplicity: 'One fire drives out one fire'. This is a sure sign of failure.

Perhaps the real key to Aufidius's speech is that he is trying to find a reason for what he knows he has to do. He has been humiliated, again, and to regain his manhood he must destroy Martius. But to do this he must find some reason. In this speech he is searching Martius's past for some clue that would justify him now. He cannot quite do it. It is with a brusque dismissal of logic that he concludes his reflections with the bare, brutal assertion:

> When, Caius, Rome is thine,
> Thou art poor'st of all: then shortly art thou mine.
> (IV.vii. 56–7)

It is the only time in the play that anyone lops off the 'Martius' from 'Caius', as if Aufidius were having a trial go at shortening the man he would like to call his own.

·5·

'O mother, mother!'

We see nothing of Martius from the moment at which Aufidius takes him into dinner in Act 4 Scene 5 until he comes out to deal with the kerfuffle that Menenius creates in the camp outside the gates of Rome. It is his longest absence from the stage and it corresponds to similar respites afforded to actor and audience in other Shakespearian tragedies at a penultimate stage of the action. This temporary 'silence' allows him all the more time to get things done, and the belatedness with which we hear about these doings helps to create the illusion that he is running out of control, that the play itself can no longer contain him.

Cominius is the key promoter of this aura, both in Act 4 Scene 6 and Act 5 Scene 1. He is the messenger of doom, a role from which he derives some comfort, or tries to:

> He is their god. He leads them like a thing
> Made by some other deity than nature,
> That shapes man better; . . .
>
> (IV.vi. 91–3)

> 'Coriolanus'
> He would not answer to; forbad all names:
> He was a kind of nothing, titleless,

96

Till he had forg'd himself a name o'th'fire
Of burning Rome.

(V.i. 11–15)

Are we to suppose that Cominius is in this latter case
reporting the actual words that Martius used—'I'll forge
myself a name . . .'? A few lines later Cominius does indeed
claim to report exactly the metaphor that Martius used, of
the grain and the chaff. But the earlier lines are spoken under
the tremor of less controlled feelings about his own
rejection, and the fantasy about Martius forging himself 'a
name o'th'fire/Of burning Rome' derives at least partly
from Cominius's own need and gift for myth-making. He is
at it again, when he rejects the suggestion that Menenius will
do any better: 'I tell you, he does sit in gold, his eye/Red as
'twould burn Rome; . . .' (V.i. 63–4).

There is a significant contrast between Cominius and
Menenius in this respect. Cominius has some robust
resources for dealing with his personal failure, and with the
prospect of Rome's doom. He can conceal from others and
perhaps from himself the pain of being rebuffed. He
maintains his dignity and takes a certain pride in doing so. It
is as if he really does believe that Rome does not deserve to
be saved. But Menenius is a softer touch, and the sequence
of scenes (V.i.; V.ii.; V.iv.) which now represents the
consequences of this softness is one of the less obvious
triumphs of the play.

So much of the play is taken up with noisy parades of self-
confidence that to find a character entertaining the fear of
failure is itself something of a relief. Our first view of
Menenius, fronting the riotous mob, had suggested an
authority in him that has progressively dissipated. The
scene after Martius's banishment marks a turning-point in
our view of him (IV.ii.). In the confrontation with the
tribunes the vengefulness is all the women's, and the fact
that Virgilia shows such an unexpected capacity for anger
makes Menenius appear particularly feeble in his efforts to

calm things down. (Middleton Murry refuses to believe that
this can be the same Virgilia we saw earlier, and redistributes
the lines accordingly.)¹ Of the poor man's sociable
invitation to supper which Volumnia so magnificently
snubs, Granville-Barker murmurs sympathetically: 'old
age's comfort in the commonplace!'² Volumnia exits with a
magisterial 'Come, come, come!' Menenius echoes this
pathetically with his 'Fie, fie, fie'.

He would like to think of himself, he would like to be
thought of by others, as Martius's father. He makes no great
demands of his little dream—until now, that is, when
circumstances force him to bring it into the open and put it
to the test. He has much more to lose than Cominius, in
whose failure he nervously foresees his own, 'grief-
shot/With . . . unkindness' (V.i. 44–5). Not for the first time
in the play, he takes refuge in the idea of a happy body. It is
plausible to believe that one of the troubles with Martius is
that he has never had enough to eat, that his blood is cold
and that the austerity with which he views his own body
makes him 'unapt/To give or to forgive' (v.i. 52–3). But it
beggars belief to imagine, as Menenius tries to do now, that a
good breakfast might change Martius's mind for him. It is
much too late to reach Martius's soul by such means, to try
and make it more supple. Martius's soul, if that is indeed
what must be touched, will have to be reached by other
routes.

Menenius is doubly humiliated. First he is shamed by the
short shrift he gets from his 'son', a humiliation exacerbated
by the taunts of the guards. But he is also humiliated by the
timing of the news that the women have succeeded where he
failed. Like Cominius before him, Menenius is shown to us
aggrandising the remorselessness of the man who has
rebuffed him (V.iv). With Sicinius for audience he can
retrieve the sense of his own dignity by magnifying
Martius's. But we have seen for ourselves the abject state to
which Menenius was reduced at the end of Act 5 Scene 2,
and we already know that the women have in fact been

successful. This means that when the news of Rome's salvation reaches the stage, poor Menenius is forced for a second time to eat his words. (Moshinsky's 1983 BBC television production saved Menenius's face by transposing Act 5 Scene 4, lines 1–33 so that they *preceded* Act 5 Scene 3.) It is a wonderfully painful moment, as we watch Menenius being forced to swallow the pride he was just beginning to take in his own failure: 'This is good news'. It is as if the play has finally erased him. It may be significant that he goes on to endow with a personal name the woman who has succeeded where he has failed: 'This Volumnia . . .' (V.iv. 53). This is the sole occasion in the play on which her name is heard. In the subsequent triumphal procession across the stage, Menenius has no part.

Martius was prepared for Menenius, and he took some pride in showing Aufidius how sternly he dealt with him. Yet it turns out that he still cares enough about Menenius that he has tried to cushion the old man's shame. Granville-Barker notes the flaw in his seemingly implacable demeanour, and goes so far as to read the 'crack'd heart' of which Martius speaks as referring to himself:

> This last old man,
> Whom with a crack'd heart I have sent to Rome, . . .
> (V.iii. 8–9)[3]

The 'crack'd heart' must primarily refer to Menenius, yet Granville-Barker's misreading is made possible by the ambiguity of the syntax, and it anticipates a truth about Martius, that his heart is not whole and entire.

We have no means of knowing the quality of resolution with which he announces that he will receive no further appeals from Rome. He speaks in general terms of refusing further embassies and suits, 'Nor from the state nor private friends' (V.iii. 18). Has it crossed his mind that he may be faced with his *family*? He may have been steeling himself against the prospect of coming face to face with wife, mother and child, or he may have succeeded in holding it at bay. Whichever we choose to believe, their entrance must catch him by surprise. In Plutarch he sees them coming a long way off, and has time to run through the gamut of his feelings before they actually arrive. But with his usual instinct for awkward timing, Shakespeare stages it so that unlike poor Menenius, the family group sails past the guards and into Martius's presence without even being announced.

Throughout a great deal of this scene, Martius is silent. But before he enters his long silence, he has a good deal to say. The sight and sound and gestures of the suppliants make speech positively flood out of him. 'Let it be virtuous to be obstinate', he grimly wails to himself, as if with the premonition that the virtues of a lifetime of obstinacy are now about to peter out.

> But out, affection!
> All bond and privilege of nature break!
> Let it be virtuous to be obstinate.
> What is that curtsy worth? or those doves' eyes,
> Which can make gods forsworn? I melt, and am not
> Of stronger earth than others. My mother bows,
> As if Olympus to a molehill should
> In supplication nod; and my young boy
> Hath an aspect of intercession which
> Great nature cries, 'Deny not'.
>
> (V.iii. 24–33)

This speech is sometimes referred to as a soliloquy. Hibbard remarks that from the two lines that precede the suppliants' entry Martius must be speaking aside, 'since the hero is not likely to reveal intimate feelings of this kind either to the Volsces or to the suppliants'.[4] But are we to suppose that Martius deliberately withholds this speech from the hearing of others? In the theatre the uncertainty can be a positive gain, in so far as the audience cannot tell whether Martius intends this speech to be 'private' or whether the occasion bereaves him of all intention. Nor can they necessarily tell exactly what the other characters hear or half-hear; Aufidius is surely straining his ears.[5] These doubts may make us feel how little 'shade' Martius can ever find, how vulnerably he stands exposed to the glare and greed of the public eye and ear, how powerful must be the feelings that force themselves into expression at such a perilous moment, when he might indeed well wish to keep them under lock and key.

Shakespeare makes Martius's obstinate denial difficult and dramatic where Plutarch's narrative is blithely predictable. Plutarch tells us that he determines at the first 'to persist in his obstinate and inflexible rancker. But overcomen in the ende with naturall affection, ... [he] yeelded to the affection of his bloode, as if he had bene violently caried with the furie of a most swift running streame'.[6] Memorably as the idea of 'great nature' resounds in Martius's voice, it is against something more than this that Shakespeare makes him struggle. The greetings that he offers in turn to his wife, his mother, Valeria and his son are notably protracted. The sheer generosity of his speech stands in abrupt contrast to the grim taciturnity that descends when he resumes his official seat to hear their request; but it also reverberates through that silence. We read into that silence the resonance of the powerful feelings to which he has given utterance: the passionate love for his wife, the tremulous reverence for his mother, the respect for Valeria, the pride in his son. Indeed passion runs through all these speeches, a passion so powerful that we wonder how he can possibly square it with the obligations embodied in the vigilant figure of Aufidius. So much for the superhuman robot.

The passion is carefully distinguished. All four of the figures whom he greets represent for him 'ideas', but they are ideas instinct with his most powerful feelings. Earlier on it seemed that for Martius the ideas of honour and valour and nobility were too pure for any individual, including himself, to be worthy of embodying them. But now he is eager to hail in these figures the living presence of ideas made flesh.

The form of words in which he assures his wife of his fidelity to her is touchingly gratuitous:

> Now by the jealous queen of heaven, that kiss
> I carried from thee, dear; and my true lip
> Hath virgin'd it e'er since.   (V.iii. 46–8)

Does he imagine that she or anyone doubts this? His loyalty towards her is almost comically at odds with the evidently more pressing question of his loyalty to Rome. Yet it is, we realise, the very idea of marital fidelity to which he is renewing his faith, an idea entirely embodied for him in the physical gesture of love. Similarly with Valeria, there is a potentially comic redundancy in his astonishingly operatic address:

> The noble sister of Publicola,
> The moon of Rome, chaste as the icicle
> That's curdied by the frost from purest snow,
> And hangs on Dian's temple! Dear Valeria!
>   (V.iii. 64–7)

In his version of the play Nahum Tate trims the image of the icicle to the simple cliché, 'Chast as the frozen Snow'.[7] This helps us to gauge the excess in Shakespeare's lines, an excess created by the dazzling intensity of Martius's admiration for the ideal of which Valeria stands as an 'epitome'. In his son too, the 'poor epitome' of himself, he foresees an idea of noble fortitude such as he might have been proud to imagine for himself. His choice of simile has nothing of the godlike or the beastly that have characterised so many of the images which others have applied to him.

> The god of soldiers,
> With the consent of supreme Jove, inform

Thy thoughts with nobleness, that thou mayst prove
To shame unvulnerable, and stick i'th'wars
Like a great sea-mark standing every flaw
And saving those that eye thee!

(V.iii. 70–5)

The clause about 'shame' is revealing.[8] In the earlier fury and turmoil he had many harsh things to say about the failure of his fellow-men to live up to his ideal of Rome, but he had little success in expressing what it was that he *loved* in 'the fundamental part of state'. His detractors accused him of pride in himself. Here he is surprised into an oblique declaration of what gives him pride in the Romans whom he loves, and in the ideas of Rome and being a Roman that they represent.

The passion which his mother inspires in him is a knottier matter. For Virgilia and Valeria and his son he feels an admiration in which he takes a justified pride. He greets them as equals. But the admiration he feels for his mother is not on the level. He marks his first recognition of her presence with a dismaying metonymy that transforms her into an abjectly impersonal formula: 'the honour'd mould/Wherein this trunk was fram'd' (V.iii. 22–3). It is not his own son that he sees 'in her hand' but 'the grandchild to her blood' (v.iii. 24). When she bows to him he transforms her gesture into one of the most memorably invidious comparisons in the play: 'As if Olympus to a molehill should/In supplication nod'. Like so many of the play's 'impossible' comparisons this would be laughable if it were not so pathetic—to find a man wishing or needing to believe that such a vertiginous scale of comparison could possibly measure a human relationship. 'Impossibility' is exactly what he tries to take refuge in, when she kneels to him and he launches into the hysterical rhetoric of apocalypse.

What's this?

Your knees to me? to your corrected son?

Then let the pebbles on the hungry beach
Fillip the stars. Then let the mutinous winds
Strike the proud cedars 'gainst the fiery sun,
Murd'ring impossibility, to make
What cannot be, slight work!

(V.iii. 56–62)

This is close to the idiom of Lear in the storm, of Macbeth in the night; here the storm and the night are all inside Martius, in his imagination.

Even more than the 'molehill', the 'gosling' gives him away: 'I'll never/Be such a gosling to obey instinct . . .'—as if the realm of 'instinct' belonged only to such tender, defenceless, pathetic creatures as 'goslings'! The 'nature' to which characters' imaginations have recourse in this play is usually a theatre of violent struggle in which the stronger destroy the weaker. Martius is both the active sponsor and the passive object of this relentless process, in which lions, bears, eagles, dragons, ospreys are unequally pitted against rats, curs, rascals, hares, geese and so on; Maurice Charney calls it a vocabulary of 'traditional primacies'.[9] The violent contrarieties of these animals are paralleled by the contrasting images of inorganic 'constancy' and organic 'softness', the admiring images of rocklike, metallic rigidity and the disparaging images of shrinking, fleshly yieldingness—a twist of silk is 'rotten', mellow fruit is ready to drop. There is little chance of escape from this regulated collective hysteria, little possibility of tolerance for the weakness of the flesh, let alone positive celebration of its tenderness. No wonder so many readers fasten on Virgilia; Menenius too, to a lesser extent, provides some relief from the relentless severity. At the margins of the savage feast there hovers the image of a creaturely frailty that human beings might choose to nurture rather than to mammock— butterflies, snails, conies, goslings, doves. Is it true that left to their own devices, the lower orders would 'feed on one another', as Martius claims (I.i. 187)? A world away, beyond the horizon of this grim vision, there glimmers the unvoiced possibility of a sociability based on collective and mutual need.

What *is* it that makes him yield to his mother—or, as we may feel, to the whole group of suppliants on behalf of whom she speaks? What does he mean when he says, 'The gods look down, and this unnatural scene/They laugh at' (v.iii. 184–5)? That it *has been* unnatural for a son and a mother to find themselves at such loggerheads? Or that it *is now* unnatural for him to yield to her, surrendering his resolution and thus being false to his own nature?

Whatever he means by it, there is an unresolvable knot of meanings in this moment. His mother is asking him to be at one and the same time true and false to his own nature: true in so far as it is his nature to do as she tells him, false in so far as it is not his nature to break a resolution. He is perfectly trapped by the fissure in the nature created by his mother's nurture. For in surrendering to her he is not just obeying nature; he is also obeying a life-long habit. Nature and custom have become so closely identified in him that in breaking away from Rome he has led the mere shadow of an existence. Now that he comes face to face with the mother who unites the double roots of his being, he is ready to melt.

Almost all the uses of the word 'nature' in the play serve to confirm the idea that it is something fixed and unalterable, particularly as it is associated with Martius himself. 'What he cannot help in his nature, you account a vice in him' (I.i. 40–1); 'Such a nature,/Tickled with good success . . .' (I.i. 258–9); 'If, as his nature is, he fall in rage . . .' (II.iii. 256); 'His nature is too noble for the world' (III.i. 252); 'Would you have me/False to my nature?' (III.ii. 14–15); 'who take it/By sovereignty of nature' (IV.vii. 34–5). 'Nature' is the habitual argument with which people try to evade or deny the demands of the will and the difficulties of choice. But at another level it is a means of contesting the power of custom.

Bacon has a couple of salutary essays which suggest the

power of custom over nature without denying its limits, 'Of Nature in Men' and 'Of Custom and Education'. 'Nature' and 'custom', he argues, are involved in a permanent process of strife and collusion, the results of which in particular lives can never with certainty be predicted. Custom's hold over nature is inherently precarious:

> Nature is often hidden, sometimes overcome, seldom extinguished . . . let not a man trust his victory over his nature too far, for nature will lay buried a great time, and yet revive upon the occasion or temptation. Like as it was with Aesop's damsel, turned from a cat to a woman, who sat very demurely at the board's end till a mouse ran before her.[10]

This comical image might remind us of the repressed gosling in Martius, which revives so belatedly 'upon the occasion or temptation'. But powerful as nature is, it is no more to be trusted than custom, its antagonist and ally. With Machiavelli for support, Bacon warns that 'there is no trusting to the force of nature nor to the bravery of words, except it be corroborate by custom'.[11] And he goes so far as to contend that:

> the predominancy of custom is everywhere visible; insomuch as a man would wonder to hear men profess, protest, engage, give great words, and then do just as they have done before; as if they were dead images and engines moved only by the wheels of custom.[12]

One can imagine the manner and matter of these reflections being brought to bear on the character and actions of Martius and the world in which he moves. Martius poses a terrible question about the relations between custom and nature. We are encouraged by other characters, and indeed by Martius himself, to think of him as a force of nature impervious to the power of custom; yet he is no less obviously a product of the power of custom, and specifically of his mother's education. He epitomises an unholy identification of the two forces, by virtue of which nature has never been thwarted by custom nor custom by nature. He has lived by this union, yet in the great confrontation with his mother he finds himself facing the embodiment of this union *in her*. He sees and feels united in her the power of great nature and the power of great custom. It is not that he is torn apart by a division in himself so much as that he finds himself standing outside the double source of his being in nature and custom, as they are embodied in his mother. He is forced to recognise that he has been torn *away* from this double source; in yielding to this recognition, he will temporarily reunite himself with it.

In Volumnia Martius faces his own and sole author. His exile from Rome has meant the severance of his ideals from the idea that they were supposed to serve. That idea survives only in fragmentary form, and it is this that lends such passion to the forms in which he addresses the three women and his son—the helpless fragments of a fatherless family. In returning to take his revenge on Rome, he seeks to punish the very ground in which that idea should have been rooted. But to see his revenge through, to see it home, he has had to forget what he owes to his own grounding: 'My birth-place hate I . . .'. And the woman who gave birth to him? And the other woman who gave birth to his own son? The Rome that Volumnia represents is the womb that gave him birth. To assault his country would mean 'treading' on his mother's womb. (We may note the ominous return of this word: Volumnia once predicted that her son would 'tread' upon Aufidius's neck [I.iii. 47], but at the end Aufidius will 'tread' upon Martius [V.vi. 133].) Volumnia manages to make it sound like a literal threat, as did Aufidius with his vow to 'wash his fierce hand' in Martius's heart. Virgilia is prompt to offer her own motherhood in support of this literal identification of the women's bodies with Rome as the motherland:

> Ay, and mine,
> That brought you forth this boy to keep your name
> Living to time.
>
> (V.iii. 125–7)

Brian Vickers is surely right to feel that there is a painfulness about Virgilia's opposition to her husband. He goes so far as to call it a betrayal: 'it is a terrible moment when Virgilia follows Volumnia's cue, when she betrays her husband and sides with the values of the patrician class'.[13] But it is not simply the values of the patrician class with which she is siding, any more than it will be simply the values of the patrician class to which Martius will yield. The idea of the family that the women represent is essential not just to the values of a particular class, but to an idea of community that transcends both personal and class affiliations. First Martius honoured the idea of Rome as an ideal community devoted to honour and virtue; now he feeds on the idea of Rome as a den of iniquity, harbouring only 'foes to nobleness'. The first he was proud to serve; now he will not rest until he has purged the second with fire.

But both ideas founder against the impossibility of purging the city of its inner divisions: first, the plebeians, now the women.[14] Much as he longed to deny their right to the name of Romans, his hatred could not rid the city of those alien creatures the multitudinous people. He had not accepted the impotence of his hatred; now he is faced with the potency of his love. He has told Menenius that he can make no exceptions. His idea of Rome is still single, uniform, absolute: it is just a different idea. But he finds it no more possible to deny the love he feels for the family he would condemn to destruction along with their fellow-Romans, than he found it possible to satisfy his hatred for the plebeians he would have evicted from his ideal city. If Virgilia has betrayed her husband, he has also betrayed her, in so far as he has abandoned the sense of what he owes to her and to their son in condemning them to death with their neighbours—or merely refused to think about it.

Aufidius had suggested that 'our virtues/Lie in the th'interpretation of the time' (IV.vii. 49–50). Volumnia echoes this phrase when she refers to 'th'interpretation of *full* time', as she points to the little boy who 'may show like all yourself' (V.iii. 69–70). Time is not just the random ebb and flow that Aufidius's phrase suggests and to which he fits his own opportunism. Volumnia impresses on her son the memory of a past and the foresight of a future to which his being is bound. It is bound by the palpable beings of the woman to whom he owes his own life and of the son to whom he has himself helped to give life. The 'interpretations' which time affords are grounded in these bonds, in the actions that forge them and the consequences that issue from them. Volumnia appeals to something which Martius has given little evidence of ever understanding or feeling, the sense of *history*, a sense both personal and public.

In making this appeal she shows no compunction in presenting the past and the future in terms calculated to make him quail at the enormity of what he owes—to her, to his wife and child, to himself. And through these, presumably, to Rome. But she makes no direct appeal to an idea of Rome to which he might be persuaded to recall his allegiance. Such an idea is now entirely incarnate in the visible, audible, tangible presence of these suppliant bodies, the women and a child. 'This is the last', Volumnia says with an unforgettable simplicity, as the group go down on their knees in the formal gesture of supplication.

It is one of the play's many formal moments. All of these occasions carry aches and embarrassments, as if Shakespeare were probing the sheer cussedness of the human nature that such formalities attempt to marshal and trim and renovate. But this is the most painful. There is nothing comical in the discomfort of this moment, as there is in varying degrees and kinds when Martius refuses the honours on the battlefield, or when he stands for the consulship, or when he seeks admission to Aufidius's hearth. Yet there is, precisely, a deep 'discomfort' in this moment. 'Comfort', in the old and strong sense of the word, is exactly what the suppliants seek from Martius. They are at his mercy; their salvation lies only in him.

There is a discomfort for the audience in the fact that the ceremony fails—as a ceremony. Not for the first time Martius fails to play his role properly. Volumnia and the others must surely go down on their knees when she says 'Down' (V.iii. 171), and it seems natural for them to rise when she says 'Come, let us go' (V.iii. 177). (Some editors insert these stage-directions.) Certainly it makes dramatic sense for Volumnia to stand up before she delivers her final withering lines.

> This fellow had a Volscian to his mother;
> His wife is in Corioles, and his child
> Like him by chance. Yet give us our dispatch:
> I am husht until our city be afire,
> And then I'll speak a little.
>
> (V.iii. 178–82)

It is a wonderful dramatic stroke to postpone the moment at which Martius yields. Comparison with Plutarch again shows how Shakespeare embarrasses the fluency of his source. There we find no awkward pauses between the end of Volumnia's speech; the gesture of collective supplication and Martius's surrender:

> And with these wordes, her selfe, his wife and children, fell downe upon their knees before him. Martius seeing that, could refraine no lenger, but went straight and lifte her up, crying out: Oh mother, what have you done to me? And holding her hard by the right hande, oh mother, sayed he.[15]

Shakespeare makes Martius seem to miss his chance: his mother's 'Come, let us go' marks the end of the ceremony.

Shakespeare also transforms the gesture that he finds in Plutarch into the most eloquent of stage-directions: 'Holds her by the hand silent'. By making it the silent prelude to speech he turns the action into something more and other than a corroboration of the words. It is as if this were itself a kind of ritual gesture which Martius suddenly invents, with what degree of impulse or deliberation we cannot tell—as if his dilemma indeed requires for its solution the intervention of a grace that bypasses words.

What happens to Martius as he holds his mother by the hand silent? Dover Wilson says confidently, 'During this silence, Coriolanus grows up, comes to know himself and to understand the meaning of life for the first time: and his reply when he speaks is his first calm, thoughtful, adult utterance in the play.'[16] There are some big words here, and it requires an act of faith to believe not only in Martius's metamorphosis but in 'the meaning of life' to the understanding of which he is suddenly supposed to ascend. Bradley also appeals to a solemn idea, though with more circumspection, when he refers to Martius's 'soul':

> To me the scene is one in which the tragic feelings of fear and pity have little place. Such anxiety as I feel is not for the fate of the hero or of any one else: it is, to use religious language, for the safety of his soul.[17]

'To use religious language': that indeed is the problem. How far can the play itself be supposed to allow, let alone positively encourage, the use of such language? Is it possible to wave aside the play's expressly pagan setting and to read into this moment religious or metaphysical convictions patently unavailable to the characters themselves? The issue here is not only the distance between what Bradley believes and what Martius could have believed, but also the distance between Bradley and Shakespeare.

It would be impertinent to dismiss out of hand Bradley's belief in Martius's soul. Even if none of the characters in the play talk about his soul—as Hamlet's and Othello's get talked about, for instance—then this does not necessarily preclude members of an audience from thinking and talking about it, whether they 'ought' to or not. In his study of Shakespeare's Roman plays, J. L. Simmons argues that their representation of a world antedating Christian revelation radically severs them from the world-view shared by Shakespeare and the audience of his time.

> Shakespeare accurately represents Rome as a pagan world in which the characters must perforce operate with no reference beyond the Earthly City. All attempts at idealistic vision by the tragic heroes, all attempts to rise above the restrictions of man and his imperfect society, are tragically affected by the absence of revelation and the real hope of glory. Implying this historical dimension, Shakespeare views his Roman world with the cosmic irony of what that world could not know.[18]

This would effectively have the audience occupying a vantage-point as high above the play as the perspective from which Martius imagines 'the gods' to be looking down and laughing at the 'unnatural scene'. It might constitute a kind of prophetic irony on Martius's part, a thwarted desire for some higher principle of providence in his world, that he should be able to imagine the justice and necessity of this perspective, while wrongly imputing it to the old, outdated pagan gods.

The burden of Simmons's argument is that Martius is a true idealist whose beliefs are necessarily baulked of realisation by the historical limits of his world. Martius represents the highest ideals of which his world is capable, the absolute equation of virtue with valour, the conception of worldly fame as man's highest goal, the impulse towards world domination. In all this he epitomises the ruling ethos of Rome itself, the Earthly City. But at the same time he embodies the contradictions within this ethos that will eventually lead to its dissolution. This has the interesting effect of making Martius's discomfort with praise, for instance, a kind of *historical* discomfort with the ethics of his world rather than evidence of his personal or social maladjustment, a mere matter of psychology. Martius becomes a bewildered idealist, striving for the absolute idealism of Christian conviction. He does not realise that he is doing this, but his audience does.

However, it is hard to believe that Shakespeare intended his immediate audience to view the play from such an exclusively Christian perspective as Simmons proposes, or even supposing that he had so intended, that they would have done so. The history of religious belief in Shakespeare's own time hardly goes far towards supporting the idea that his audience would have enjoyed a sense of their own unanimity over the question of what constituted a 'Christian perspective'. Some of them might even have felt more kinship with the benighted pagans on stage than with some of their own Christian contemporaries. In any case there is reason to believe that so far from reposing in a sense of the difference between a pagan then and a Christian now, Shakespeare and his audience were impressed by the powerful analogies that could be drawn between them (as Huffman's work on the 'context' of the play demonstrates). The history of Shakespearian criticism is littered with attempts to provide èxactly that authoritative perspective from which the conflicts which the plays dramatise can be clarified, and safely viewed at an ironical distance. Thus recently, for example, Terry Eagleton, for whom Coriolanus can be viewed in historical terms as the embodiment of a political future, 'perhaps Shakespeare's most developed study of a bourgeois individualist'.[19]

Shakespeare and his audience may be presumed to have believed and thought a variety of things about Roman history and Christian historiography, and it seems improbable that as the dramatic possibilities inherent in the story of Coriolanus began to dawn on Shakespeare, he harboured the singleness of motive that Simmons ascribes to him. It is more likely that from time to time Shakespeare noticed that the language he gave his characters to speak, and the situations they found themselves in, carried echoes of Christian values and meanings which he was powerless to expunge even if he had wanted to—words such as 'grace', 'gracious' and 'graceful', for instance. Emrys Jones observes that the supplication scene carries a strange and unexpected resemblance to the visit of the three Marys to Christ's tomb.[20] But Jones cites this and other examples of the play's odd echoes of the Gospel narratives not as evidence for a hidden level of Christian meaning, so much as evidence for the predatory power of Shakespeare's imagination, ceaselessly reworking the material of collective memory—the source of his success as a great popular dramatist.

'O mother, mother!' The local belatedness with which Martius is too late to complete the ceremony enacts in miniature the larger tragic belatedness of his whole life:

> O mother, mother!
> What have you done? Behold, the heavens do ope,
> The gods look down, and this unnatural scene
> They laugh at. O my mother, mother! O!
> You have won a happy victory to Rome;
> But for your son, believe it, O, believe it,
> Most dangerously you have with him prevail'd,
> If not most mortal to him. But let it come.
>
> (V.iii. 182–9)

Bradley says that 'it lies in his nature that his deepest and most sacred feeling, that for his mother, is almost dumb'.[21] Almost, but not quite: Shakespeare wonderfully creates the sense of this 'depth' by giving him the repeated 'O's'. Even more important is the tiny transformation of 'O mother, mother!' into 'O my mother, mother! O!' This beautifully alters an unambiguous vocative into a more mysterious

exclamation. For the 'my' has the strange effect of distancing
her from him, as if he were thinking of her in the second and
third persons at one and the same time, both as 'thou' and
'that mother of mine'. The sense of the distance between
them at this moment of intimacy is carried further when he
goes on to speak of *himself* in the third person: 'But for your
son . . . Most dangerously you have with him prevail'd,/If
not most mortal to him'. The wording makes it seem as if he
is abandoning the sense of his own agency, transferring it all
to her—or, in the culmination of the desolate slide of
pronouns, 'it': 'But let it come'. When he then turns to
Aufidius, he repeats Aufidius's name no less than three
times, as if seeking in vain for reassurance that Aufidius still
thinks him for the man he is. Granville-Barker notes well of
these repetitions and the 'varying cadence' an actor can give
them, that they represent 'all the pleading on his own
behalf—it is little!—that Marcius' pride could ever let him
make'.[22] It is more than his honour and his mercy that have
been set 'at difference' in him.

Martius's is not the only mysterious 'depth' in this scene.
Does Volumnia understand her son's prophetic hint when
he says, 'if not most mortal to him'? Because she says
nothing else in this scene (or nothing that we can hear—it is
possible that Martius exchanges some private words with
the women, while Aufidius speaks his brief aside (V.iii.
199–201)), some readers assume that she does not
understand. She cares only for Rome, and she will return in
triumph to be hailed as 'the life of Rome': for her and Rome
it is a 'comic' ending. But we cannot tell what Volumnia
does or does not understand and feel about her triumph.
We hear nothing from her or from the other women for the
rest of the play. Again we can see Shakespeare creating a
positive reticence, by omitting to provide her with a
reaction to her son's ominous prophecy. In Alexandre
Hardy's *Coriolan* nothing is left unspoken as the son
magnificently announces to his mother that she should not
expect to see him again until they meet 'en l'Hérébique

salle'. With this chilling flourish he bids her farewell, leaving her to close the great scene thus:

> Hélas! de ce soupçon tu me navres le coeur.
> O Dieux! Grands Dieux du Ciel! faites qu'il soit
>   mocqueur.[23]

After the fugitive reverberations of the supplication scene, the unbridled noise that greets 'the recomforted' women on their return to Rome makes a shattering contrast. In the formal welcome accorded the women, the senator urges his listeners to 'unshout the noise that banish'd Martius' (V.v. 4). How do you 'unshout' something? It is a generous and improbable idea, and it stands little chance of a hearing amidst the pure din into which the life of Rome is disappearing. It is the last we see and hear of Rome: the sight and sound of public triumph.

Martius has chosen to return with Aufidius to face a different music. It is noticeable that Aufidius shows some hesitation in steeling himself for the job in hand. His hurried instructions to the attendants betray his nervous excitement:

> Bid them repair to th'market-place, where I,
> Even in theirs and in the commons' ears,
> Will vouch the truth of it. Him I accuse
> The city ports by this hath enter'd, . . .
>
>   (V.vi. 3–6)

There is a horribly awkward half-rhyme on 'theirs' and 'ears', and a grotesque contortion in the throttled syntax of 'Him I accuse'. The conspirators will help him wrench himself up, as he rehearses the history of his relations with Martius. Twice he seems to interrupt them as they set him going on a new track (v.vi. 29, 44). As the sound of Martius's triumphal entry reaches the stage, the three conspirators join forces by speaking for the first time in uninterrupted sequence (V.vi. 50–9). Aufidius will not be up to managing this feat on his own. He will not be able to say, 'Alone I did it'.

Some readers express disappointment with Martius's entry speech in this scene (V.vi. 71–84). It is difficult to believe that his heart is in the routine words of self-justification with which he offers his official report to his employers, the Volscian lords. At the end of the supplication scene he had asked Aufidius to 'stand to' him, as if knowing that he would have some explaining to do. It may be that he is just going through the motions now, listlessly waiting to be denounced. (But does he expect to be denounced by *Aufidius*?) It may even be that in a strange way he positively wants to receive judgement. We remember that when he offered his throat to Aufidius he expected either to receive 'fair justice' or to do him 'service' (IV.iv. 25).

The justice that he receives from Aufidius is certainly not fair. One of the Volscian lords tries desperately to plead the case for a 'judicious hearing' (V.vi. 126), echoing the vain efforts of Menenius and the nameless Roman senator to get Martius dealt with by 'lawful form' (III.i. 320–6). It is too late. Aufidius has roused a 'Coriolanus' whom the people of Corioles remember all too well, the monstrous enemy who killed their sons and daughters and cousins and fathers, the man who has destroyed their *families*. It is an image painfully at odds with the humbled and resigned man whom we saw for ourselves being tenderly reunited with his own family. Aufidius stage-manages the abrupt revival of the proud, touchy, magnificent warrior. As with our last views of Othello and Lear and Macbeth, Martius is gathered up by the final surge of an earlier and simpler self.

There is a cunning blend of truth and falsehood in Aufidius's cruel jibe 'thou boy of tears!' (V.vi. 101). There has all along been something in Martius of the boy who has not grown up, never freed himself from his mother's apron strings. But that boy, the boy who relished the derring-do of battle and his mother's praises, was precisely not a boy of *tears*. Tears were what he left behind him, in both senses, in that he left them behind with his mother's milk when she pushed him out to the wars, and in that they were what he left his victims with. The 'boy' himself was a boy of iron self-control. It was more than his upper-lip that was stiff: rigidity was his defining attribute. The tears that he shed in the moment of yielding to his mother were those of the boy he had never been, and in shedding them then, he discovered what might have made him more of a human being in being less of a 'man'.

Aufidius's 'boy' touches him to the quick in suggesting that he is not the impregnable man he was brought up to believe himself. At least he has a quick to be touched. It launches him into the glorious and justly famous lines with which he invites his death at the hands of the enemies who afforded him his greatest triumph.

> Cut me to pieces, Volsces, men and lads,
> Stain all your edges on me. Boy! False hound!
> If you have writ your annals true, 'tis there,
> That like an eagle in a dove-cote, I
> Flutter'd your Volscians in Corioles.
> Alone I did it. Boy!
>
> (V.vi. 111–16)

Moralistic critics have been known to complain that Martius never learns through his suffering as they suppose tragic characters are supposed to. But in the theatre at least, any actor worth his salt should make it impossible to entertain such reflections. An audience must be exhilarated by the lines that begin 'If you have writ your annals true', the soaring trajectory that lands with such a delightful surprise on the contemptuously delicate—'Flutter'd'. He is in his element once more, alone against a hostile multitude: he must be happy, in his own way.

But his death is bound to be shocking. Tynan preserves

the unforgettably spectacular way that Olivier managed it in 1959—on 'a promontory some twelve feet above the stage, from which he topples forward, to be caught by the ankles so that he dangles, inverted, like the slaughtered Mussolini'.[24] The ending of the play itself is shockingly precipitate. Does it represent a miscalculation on Shakespeare's part? Many critics have wished it different, and one can find some interesting proposals to soften the sheer abruptness of Shakespeare's ending. Its most disconcerting feature is that it takes place not in Rome but in Corioles (or Antium—the location changes halfway through the scene); or more to the point, that we never hear and see what Rome makes of the news of Martius's death. Kitto quite frankly describes the alternative ending he finds himself expecting—it is rather impressive:

> Shakespeare was on the verge of inventing a really great and dramatic ending: let the Senate, with the full support of Tribunes and People, solemnly decree the honourable recall of the great hero, and then let the enthusiastic acclamations be suddenly hushed with the news that he has been murdered in Corioli.[25]

This would certainly serve them right, and it testifies to a feeling of unsatisfied vengeance that many readers seem to feel: Rome should not get off so lightly. More particularly, there is a scene missing that belongs, one may feel, to Volumnia—exactly the scene that we find in Hardy's version, which has her receive the news of her son's death and indulge in a good deal of vociferous guilt: 'O Mère parricide! o Mère criminelle!' and so on.[26]

Tate's version is also interesting, not so much for the ludicrously convenient orchestration which allows Martius to survive long enough to watch Aufidius die, Virgilia die from the mortal wound she has given herself to avoid being raped by Aufidius, Volumnia enter with the tortured and mutilated little Martius under one arm and exit (mad) having killed the villainous Nigridius—not so much for all this nonsense, as for the fulfilment of the fantasy that Martius be reunited with his family.[27] What Tate does in effect is to arrange an impeccable funeral tableau: Martius dies with his wife under one arm and his son under the other, the perfect family man. Absurd as this is, it helps to focus exactly what is so desolate about Shakespeare's ending. The reunion of Martius with his family in the great supplication scene arouses deep and complicated feelings. These are then abandoned and stranded by the final scene in Antium/Corioles.

There is also a problem about Aufidius, or really the culmination of his problematic role in the play and his relationship with Martius. Bradley identifies Aufidius as 'by far the weakest spot in the drama'. Shakespeare has given him too little substance to bear the weight of the contrast with Martius: 'he is a man of straw. He was wanted merely for the plot, and in reading some passages in his talk we seem to see Shakespeare yawning as he wrote'. It is slightly surprising then to find this man of straw rousing Bradley to such fierce indignation in the final scene of the play:

> Such an emotion as mere disgust is out of place in a tragic close; but I confess I feel nothing but disgust as Aufidius speaks the last words, except some indignation with the poet who allowed him to speak them, and an unregenerate desire to see the head and body of the speaker lying on opposite sides of the stage.[28]

This is a pleasantly candid confession. Bradley's 'unregenerate desire' for vengeance does point to the absence of something from Shakespeare's ending. Bradley would like to see Aufidius pay, just as Kitto wanted to see Rome pay. Justice has not been done, and the reader has to take the law into his own hands. For his 1963 Nottingham production Tyrone Guthrie invented an interesting ending, that had Aufidius crooning a 'wordless elegy' over his dead rival.[29] This image of grief and reparation is a revealing one—again, as it points to a desire for something in the scene which the text does not itself provide. Guthrie's Aufidius is, as it were, seeking to appease Bradley's wrath.

It is not necessary to conclude that Aufidius is a man of straw, nor that his behaviour in the closing scene is simply disgusting. It is possible but it is not necessary to believe that he is simply cynical, in that he has planned all along to bump off his rival and then just apologise:

> My rage is gone,
> And I am struck with sorrow.
>
> (V.vi. 146–7)

—the very simplicity of the words allows the actor a huge range of intention and intonation. It is impossible to measure his sincerity.

What is there to say after all? It has all been said, over and over again, everything that there is to say about this hypnotic, infuriating, calamitous person, Caius Martius Coriolanus. He has exhausted everyone's patience and powers of speech. It is honourable of Aufidius not to make more of an effort than he does, and he strikes a more tactful note than he is usually given credit for doing, in the beautifully muted rhythm of the line: 'Beat thou the drum that it speak mournfully' (V.vi. 149).

There is an appropriately speechless eloquence to the 'dead march' that Aufidius calls for and that the stage-directions carefully specify. Martius's death has had about it both a shamefulness and a magnificence; and so has his whole life. In the instant of its aftermath, the sheer dumb neutrality of the dead march is not unwelcome, and as its steady pulse-beats gradually fade from the theatre, their simple dignity eases the passage of Martius into our memories. He and his play will not be easy guests there, but they will certainly be permanent lodgers: 'sprightly walking, audible, and full of vent'.

Notes

PREFACE

1. Laurence Kitchin, *Mid-Century Drama* (London: Faber & Faber, 1960), p. 149. For another vivid account of Olivier's performance, see Kenneth Tynan, *Tynan on Theatre* (Harmondsworth: Penguin, 1964), pp. 94–6.
2. Kitchin, p. 148.

CHAPTER 1

1. J. Middleton Murry, 'A Neglected Heroine of Shakespeare', *Countries of the Mind* (London: Collins, 1922), p. 54.
2. Norman Rabkin, *Shakespeare and the Common Understanding* (Chicago and London: University of Chicago Press, 1967), p. 122.
3. Robert S. Miola, *Shakespeare's Rome* (Cambridge: Cambridge University Press, 1983), p. 166.
4. For sympathetic and perceptive accounts of the 'mob's' behaviour, see Anne Barton, 'Livy, Machiavelli, and Shakespeare's *Coriolanus*', *Shakespeare Survey* 38 (1985), pp. 117–18; Jonathan Dollimore, *Radical Tragedy:*

Religion, Ideology and Power in the Drama of Shakespeare and his Contemporaries (Brighton: Harvester Press, 1984), pp. 222–4; and Wilbur Sanders in Wilbur Sanders and Howard Jacobson, *Shakespeare's Magnanimity: Four Tragic Heroes, Their Friends and Families* (London: Chatto & Windus, 1978), pp. 138–40.

5. Bertolt Brecht, 'Study of the First Scene of Shakespeare's *Coriolanus*', *Brecht on Theatre: The Development of an Aesthetic*, ed. and tr. John Willett (New York: Hill & Wang, London: Eyre Methuen, 1978), p. 252.

6. John W. Velz, 'The Ancient World in Shakespeare: Authenticity or Anachronism? A Retrospect', *Shakespeare Survey* 31 (1978), p. 12. See also Velz, 'Cracking Strong Curbs Asunder: Roman Destiny and the Roman Hero in *Coriolanus*', *English Literary Renaissance* 13 (1983), pp. 58–69.

7. Michael Goldman makes some excellent points about the characteristic syntactical effects created by Martius's 'pursuit of the delayed idea', in *Acting and Action in Shakespearean Tragedy* (Princeton, NJ: Princeton University Press, 1985), pp. 150–4. Madeleine Doran notes the importance to the play of disabling comparisons which simultaneously augment and diminish, in *Shakespeare's Dramatic Language* (Madison, Wisc., and London: University of Wisconsin Press, 1976), p. 192.

8. John Walter and Keith Wrightson, 'Dearth and the Social Order in Early Modern England', *Rebellion, Popular Protest and the Social Order in Early Modern England*, ed. Paul Slack (Cambridge: Cambridge University Press, 1984), p. 108.

9. *Ibid.*, p. 114.

10. *Ibid.*, p. 128.

11. Reuben Brower, introduction to *Coriolanus*, Signet Shakespeare edition (New York and Toronto: New

American Library; London: New English Library, 1966), pp. xxxv–vi.

12. M.J.B. Allen, 'Toys, Prologues and the Great Amiss: Shakespeare's Tragic Openings', *Stratford-upon-Avon Studies, 20: Shakespearian Tragedy* (London: Edward Arnold, 1984), p. 16.

13. A.C. Bradley, *Coriolanus*, Second Annual Shakespeare Lecture, *Proceedings of the British Academy* (1911–12), p. 469.

14. H.D.F. Kitto, *Poiesis: Structure and Thought* (Berkeley and Los Angeles: University of California Press; London: Cambridge University Press, 1966), pp. 377–8.

15. David G. Hale, '*Coriolanus*: The Death of a Political Metaphor', *Shakespeare Quarterly* 22 (1971), pp. 197–202.

16. Geoffrey Bullough (ed.), *Narrative and Dramatic Sources of Shakespeare* (London: Routledge & Kegan Paul, and New York: Columbia University Press, 1964), vol. 5, p. 552. All references in the text to 'Plutarch' refer to 'The Life of Caius Martius Coriolanus' in Sir Thomas North's translation of *Plutarch's Lives of the Noble Grecians and Romanes* (1579), as reprinted by Bullough.

17. *Coriolanus*, ed. Philip Brockbank, New Arden Shakespeare (London: Methuen, 1976), p. 105.

18. See Doran, pp. 189–91.

19. Carol M. Sicherman makes some good points about the play's use of proverbs, and Martius's 'preceptive habit of mind', in '*Coriolanus*: The Failure of Words', *English Literary History* 39 (June 1972), p. 197.

20. See Sanders in Sanders and Jacobson, pp. 141–2.

21. Bullough, p. 527.

22. *Ibid.*, p. 505.

23. *Ibid.*, p. 506.

24. *Ibid.*, p. 508.

25. See Janet Adelman's interesting psychoanalytic account, ' "Anger's My Meat": Feeding, Dependency,

and Aggression in *Coriolanus*', in *Shakespeare: Pattern of Excelling Nature*, ed. David Bevington and Jay L. Halio (Newark: University of Delaware Press, 1978), pp. 108–24; also, for the specific connection of *Macbeth* and *Coriolanus*, Coppélia Kahn, *Man's Estate: Masculine Identity in Shakespeare* (Berkeley and Los Angeles: University of California Press, 1981), pp. 151–92, and Linda Bamber, *Comic Women, Tragic Men: A Study of Gender and Genre in Shakespeare* (Stanford: Stanford University Press, 1982), pp. 91–107.

26. This line of thought was suggested by Irene Worth's wonderful Volumnia in Elijah Moshinsky's 1983 BBC television production of the play.

27. Bullough, p. 512.

28. William Empson, *Essays on Shakespeare*, ed. David Pirie (Cambridge: Cambridge University Press, 1986), pp. 177–83.

29. *Ibid.*, p. 178.

30. *Ibid.*, p. 177.

31. Paul A. Cantor develops an interesting argument about the importance of 'spiritedness' to the ethos of Rome, the word being intended to stand for the Greek *thumos*, in *Shakespeare's Rome: Republic and Empire* (Ithaca, NY, and London: Cornell University Press, 1976), pp. 37ff, and note 17, p. 213.

32. The only other occasion on which he does so is at III.ii.103, when he refers to 'This mould of Martius'.

CHAPTER 2

1. 'Cato's' is Theobald's emendation for the Folio's inexplicable 'Calues'.

2. *The Complete Poems and Plays of T. S. Eliot* (London: Faber & Faber, 1969), p. 127.

3. Rabkin, pp. 129–32.

4. *Ibid.*, p. 131.

5. See Sanders in Sanders and Jacobson, p. 149.
6. Brockbank has a valuable note, Arden edn., pp. 144–6.
7. Paul A. Jorgensen has some useful things to say about Shakespeare's representation of the sounds of war, in Chapter 1 of *Shakespeare's Military World* (Berkeley and Los Angeles: University of California Press, 1956), pp. 1–34.
8. See D. J. Gordon's justly renowned essay, 'Name and Fame: Shakespeare's Coriolanus', *Papers Mainly Shakespearian*, ed. G. I. Duthie (Edinburgh and London: Oliver & Boyd, 1964), pp. 40–57.
9. Martin Spevack's *Harvard Concordance to Shakespeare* (Cambridge, Mass.: Harvard University Press, 1973) gives 'Martius' a count of seventy-nine and 'Coriolanus' thirty-four . Brockbank notes that most editors change the speech-heading from 'Mar.' to 'Cor.' when he gets his new name, but that the Folio retains 'Mar.' until he gets back to Rome (Arden edn. p. 147).
10. Bullough, p. 515.
11. Joyce Van Dyke notes of Martius's habits of speech: 'In grammatical terms he is a man who omits conjunctions, but this syntactical characteristic penetrates his habits of feeling and perception as well . . .' ('Making a Scene: Language and Gesture in *Coriolanus*', *Shakespeare Survey* 30 [1977], p. 136).
12. Editors note that Joseph Hall's *Characters of Vices and Virtues* was published in 1608, starting off what G.R. Hibbard calls 'something of a literary craze' (*Coriolanus*, New Penguin Shakespeare, Harmondsworth: Penguin Books, 1967, p. 207).
13. John Bayley, *Shakespeare and Tragedy* (London, Boston and Henley: Routledge & Kegan Paul, 1981), p. 158.
14. The Folio blurs the transition by printing this passage as five lines of verse, though only the last two extend to full pentameters. Modern editions return the first three lines to prose.
15. A point made by Gail Kern Paster, 'To Starve with

Feeding: The City in *Coriolanus*', *Shakespeare Studies* 11 (1978), p. 127.

16. Cantor emphasises that 'no single attitude toward Rome prevailed in the English Renaissance, for many of the great intellectual conflicts of the age had a way of focusing precisely on Rome as a point of dispute' (*Shakespeare's Rome*, p. 17). For further detailed discussion of some of the contemporary disputes for which this play provides hospitality, see W. Gordon Zeefeld, '*Coriolanus* and Jacobean Politics', *Modern Language Review* 57 (1962), pp. 321–34, and more extendedly, Clifford Chalmers Huffman, *Coriolanus in Context* (Lewisburg: Bucknell University Press, 1971).
17. Arguments well marshalled by Barton in 'Livy, Machiavelli, and Shakespeare's *Coriolanus*'.
18. Brockbank, introduction to Arden edn, p. 59.
19. Lawrence Danson rightly stresses the unusual prominence in this play of the figures of metonymy and synecdoche, and draws some useful conclusions about the role in the play as a whole of these 'figures of fragmentation and usurpation', in *Tragic Alphabet: Shakespeare's Drama of Language* (New Haven and London: Yale University Press, 1974), p. 143.
20. See Julian Glover's comments, in J. R. Mulryne, '*Coriolanus* at Stratford-upon-Avon: Three Actors' Remarks', *Shakespeare Quarterly* 29 (1978), p. 331.
21. Tynan, p. 94.
22. Paster, p. 123.

CHAPTER 3

1. See Danson, pp. 148–50.
2. Bayley, p. 151.
3. Harley Granville-Barker, *Prefaces to Shakespeare* (London: Batsford, 1958), vol. 2, p. 289.
4. William Hazlitt, notice in *The Examiner*, 15 December

1816, repr. in *A View of the English Stage* (1818), *The Complete Works of William Hazlitt*, ed. P. P. Howe (London and Toronto: Dent, 1934), vol. 5, p. 350. This review formed the basis for Hazlitt's outraged and outrageous account of the play's political bias in the relevant chapter of *Characters of Shakespear's Plays* (1817), *Complete Works*, vol. 4, pp. 214–21.

5. Danson, p. 2.
6. As Dollimore, for example, argues in *Radical Tragedy*, pp. 218–30.
7. Cantor, p. 115.
8. Michèle Willems draws some shrewd parallels between Martius and the populace in this respect, '*Coriolan* ou la parole devaluée', *Travaux de l'Université de Toulouse-Le Mirail*, Série B, Tome 5 (1984), pp. 126–9.
9. Bullough, p. 518.
10. Adelman observes that 'Behind Coriolanus's rage at the plebeians . . . stands the specter of his own hunger and his own fear of dependence' (' "Anger's My Meat" ', p. 115; see also note 6, p. 120); Kahn pursues some of these suggestions in *Man's Estate*, especially pp. 162–3.
11. Lionel Trilling, *Speaking of Literature and Society*, ed. Diana Trilling (New York and London: Harcourt Brace Jovanovich, 1980), p. 263.
12. *Ibid.*, p. 262.
13. A. P. Rossiter, *Angel with Horns, and other Shakespeare Lectures*, ed. Graham Storey (London: Longmans, 1961), p. 243.
14. Brian Vickers, *Shakespeare: Coriolanus* (London: Edward Arnold, 1976), p. 30.
15. J.C.F. Littlewood, '*Coriolanus* (II)', *Cambridge Quarterly* 3 (1967–8), p. 31.
16. Rabkin, p. 140.
17. *Ibid.*, p. 142.
18. Littlewood, pp. 33–50.
19. As Littlewood argues, for example: '*Coriolanus*', *Cambridge Quarterly* 2 (1966–7), p. 351.

20. Empson, p. 182.
21. *Ibid.*, p. 182.
22. Brockbank's note, Arden edn., p. 200.
23. Huffman, p. 148.
24. Geoffrey Hill, ' "The True Conduct of Human Judgment": Some Observations on *Cymbeline*', *The Lords of Limit: Essays on Literature and Ideas* (London: Andre Deutsch, 1984), pp. 55–66.
25. Huffman, p. 195.
26. Brockbank shrewdly notes the possibility of 'the pressure of one word upon the other, with some contact of sound, usage, and sense' (Brockbank's note, Arden edn, p. 221).
27. Kitchin, p. 146.
28. *Ibid.*, p. 146.
29. Caedmon recording, directed by Howard Sackler, The Shakespeare Recording Society, Inc. 1962.
30. Kitchin, p. 148.

CHAPTER 4

1. Emrys Jones, *Scenic Form in Shakespeare* (Oxford: Oxford University Press, 1971), p. 81. This is a long play, and it is possible to take an interval after Act 1, as well as later. Terry Hands's 1977–9 Royal Shakespeare Company production took this option.
2. Granville-Barker, p. 241.
3. Katherine Stockholder, for example, writes 'Shakespeare underscores his inability to confront himself by what might be called a missing scene—the interval between the time of his banishment and his appearance in Corioles, a time structurally correspondent to the scenes in *King Lear* in which Lear finds a new image in "unaccommodated man." ' ('The Other Coriolanus', *PMLA*, 85 [1970], p. 231). For a more

generous account of this phase of Martius's career, see
Sanders, *Shakespeare's Magnanimity*, pp. 161–2.

4. Van Dyke, p. 143.
5. Bullough, p. 526.
6. *Ibid.*
7. *Ibid.*, p. 527.
8. *Ibid.*
9. Arnold van Gennep, *The Rites of Passage*, tr. Monika B.
   Vizedom and Gabrielle L. Caffee (London: Routledge
   & Kegan Paul, 1960), p. 26.
10. Granville-Barker, vol. 2, p. 245.
11. Bamber draws some interesting parallels between
    Martius and Macbeth as regards their commitment to
    repetition: 'The compulsion to repeat is a function of
    the absence of the Other' (Bamber, p. 97).
12. Bullough, p. 531.
13. Kitchin, p. 144.
14. Hazlitt, vol. 4, p. 256. It was a claim that Hazlitt himself
    made good in his detailed descriptions of Kean's
    performances.
15. Miola notes the importance of the gestures of
    handclasping and kneeling throughout the Roman
    plays; in this play, 'both represent civilized rituals of
    interaction that contrast sharply with the Roman
    business of warmaking' (Miola, p. 195).
16. Hibbard, p. 241.˙
17. Goldman observes of this speech, 'The main effect is
    that the attempt to characterize becomes tangled and
    chokes on itself'; and further, 'Coriolanus's character
    has something to do with the way other people choke
    on it' (Goldman, pp. 145, 146).

CHAPTER 5

1. J. Middleton Murry, pp. 48–9. Rabkin observes that
   'Virgilia's cold unblinking hostility comes as such a

surprise to us that we are forced to re-evaluate her character' (Rabkin, p. 126).

2. Granville-Barker, vol. 2, p. 241.

3. *Ibid.*, p. 261.

4. Hibbard, p. 248.

5. A similar doubt affects Martius's lines: 'Like a dull actor now/I have forgot my part and I am out,/Even to a full disgrace' (V.iii.40–2). Hibbard marks these as 'aside' (Hibbard, p. 173); Brockbank says that he 'presumably speaks reflectively and aside' (Brockbank's note, Arden edn, p. 288); but Maurice Charney assumes that he is confessing his weakness directly to Virgilia (*Shakespeare's Roman Plays: The Function of Imagery in the Drama*, Cambridge, Mass.: Harvard University Press, 1961, p. 176).

6. Bullough, pp. 538–9.

7. Nahum Tate, *The Ingratitude of a Common-Wealth: Or, the Fall of Caius Martius Coriolanus* (1682); extracts reprinted in Brian Vickers (ed.), *Shakespeare: The Critical Heritage*, vol. 1, 1623–92 (London and Boston: Routledge & Kegan Paul, 1974), here p. 393.

8. Brockbank writes finely of the 'immense resonance' of these lines, in the introduction to his Arden edn, pp. 56–7; so too does Barton, 'Livy, Marchiavelli and Shakespeare's *Coriolanus*', p. 128.

9. Charney, p. 169. Other critics who have written about the play's animal imagery include G. Wilson Knight, *The Imperial Theme: Further Interpretations of Shakespeare's Tragedies including the Roman Plays*, 3rd edn (London: Methuen, 1951), pp. 163–5; J. C. Maxwell, 'Animal Imagery in *Coriolanus*', *Modern Language Review* 42 (1947), pp. 417–21; and Paster, 'To Starve with Feeding', pp. 135–7.

10. Francis Bacon, 'Of Nature in Men', *The Essays*, ed. John Pitcher (Harmondsworth: Penguin 1985), pp. 177–8.

11. Bacon, 'Of Custom and Education', p. 179.

12. *Ibid.*, p. 179.

13. Vickers, p. 46.
14. Bamber makes an important suggestion about Martius's hatred of the plebeians when she says, 'This is the kind of irrational fury that the other heroes seem to reserve for their women' (Bamber, p. 104).
15. Bullough, pp. 540–1.
16. John Dover Wilson, introduction to *Coriolanus*, New Cambridge edn (Cambridge: Cambridge University Press, 1960), p. xxxiv.
17. Bradley, p. 467.
18. J. L. Simmons, *Shakespeare's Pagan World: The Roman Tragedies* (Charlottesville: University of Virginia Press, 1973; Brighton: Harvester Press, 1974), p. 8.
19. Terry Eagleton, *William Shakespeare* (Oxford and New York: Blackwell, 1986), p. 73.
20. Emrys Jones, *The Origins of Shakespeare* (Oxford: Oxford University Press, 1977), p. 65.
21. Bradley, p. 459.
22. Granville-Barker, vol. 2, p. 291.
23. Alexandre Hardy, *Coriolan* (1625), ed. Terence Allott (Exeter: University of Exeter Press, 1978), 1075–6.
24. Tynan, p. 95.
25. Kitto, p. 389.
26. Hardy, 1325ff.
27. Tate, vol. 1, pp. 399–406.
28. Bradley, p. 470. ˙
29. Ralph Berry, 'The Metamorphoses of *Coriolanus*', *Shakespeare Quarterly* 26 (1975), p. 182.

Bibliography

EDITIONS

New Arden Shakespeare edition, ed. Philip Brockbank, London: Methuen, 1976.

New Cambridge Shakespeare edition, ed. John Dover Wilson, Cambridge: Cambridge University Press, 1960.

New Penguin Shakespeare edition, ed. G. R. Hibbard, Harmondsworth: Penguin Books, 1967.

Signet Shakespeare edition, ed. Reuben Brower, New York and Toronto: New American Library, and London: New English Library, 1966.

CRITICISM

Adelman, Janet, ' "Anger's My Meat": Feeding, Dependency, and Aggression in *Coriolanus*', in *Shakespeare: Pattern of Excelling Nature*, ed. David Bevington and Jay L. Halio, Newark: University of Delaware Press, 1978, pp. 108–24.

Bamber, Linda, *Comic Women, Tragic Men: A Study of Gender and Genre in Shakespeare*, Stanford: Stanford University Press, 1982.

Barton, Anne, 'Livy, Machiavelli, and Shakespeare's *Coriolanus*', *Shakespeare Survey* 38 (1985), pp. 115–29.

Bayley, John, *Shakespeare and Tragedy*, London, Boston and Henley: Routledge & Kegan Paul, 1981.

Berry, Ralph, 'The Metamorphoses of *Coriolanus*', *Shakespeare Quarterly* 26 (1975), pp. 172–83.

Bradley, A. C., '*Coriolanus*', Second Annual Shakespeare Lecture, *Proceedings of the British Academy* (1911–12), pp. 457–73.

Brecht, Bertolt, 'Study of the First Scene of Shakespeare's *Coriolanus*', *Brecht on Theatre: The Development of an Aesthetic*, ed. and tr. John Willett, New York: Hill & Wang; London: Eyre Methuen, 1978, pp. 252–65.

Brockman, B. A. (ed.), *Coriolanus: A Casebook*, London and Basingstoke: Macmillan, 1977.

Brower, Reuben A., *Hero and Saint: Shakespeare and the Graeco-Roman Heroic Tradition*, Oxford: Oxford University Press, 1971.

Bullough, Geoffrey, *Narrative and Dramatic Sources of Shakespeare*, London: Routledge & Kegan Paul; New York: Columbia University Press, 1964, Vol. 5, pp. 453–563.

Calderwood, James L., '*Coriolanus*: Wordless Meanings and Meaningless Words', *Studies in English Literature* 6 (1966), pp. 211–24.

Cantor, Paul A., *Shakespeare's Rome: Republic and Empire*, Ithaca, NY, and London: Cornell University Press, 1976.

Charney, Maurice, *Shakespeare's Roman Plays: The Function of Imagery in the Drama*, Cambridge, Mass.: Harvard University Press, 1961.

Daniell, David, '*Coriolanus*' in Europe, London: Athlone Press, 1980.

Danson, Lawrence, *Tragic Alphabet: Shakespeare's Drama of Language*, New Haven and London: Yale University Press, 1974.

Dollimore, Jonathan, *Radical Tragedy: Religion, Ideology and*

Power in the Drama of Shakespeare and His Contemporaries, Brighton: Harvester Press, 1984.

Doran, Madeleine, *Shakespeare's Dramatic Language*, Madison, Wisc. and London: University of Wisconsin Press, 1976.

Empson, William, *Essays on Shakespeare*, ed. David Pirie, Cambridge: Cambridge University Press, 1986.

Fish, Stanley, *Is There a Text in This Class?: The Authority of Interpretive Communities*, Cambridge, Mass. and London: Harvard University Press, 1980, pp. 197–245.

Goldman, Michael, *Acting and Action in Shakespearean Tragedy*, Princeton, NJ : Princeton University Press, 1985.

Gordon, D. J., 'Name and Fame: Shakespeare's Coriolanus', *Papers Mainly Shakespearian*, ed. G. I. Duthie, Edinburgh and London: Oliver & Boyd, 1964, pp. 40–57.

Granville-Barker, Harley, *Prefaces to Shakespeare*, London: Batsford, 1958, vol. 2, pp. 150–299.

Gurr, Andrew, 'Coriolanus and the Body Politic', *Shakespeare Survey* 28 (1975), pp. 63–9.

Hale, David G., 'Coriolanus: The Death of a Political Metaphor', *Shakespeare Quarterly* 22 (1971), pp. 197–202.

Hardy, Alexandre, *Coriolan* (1625), ed. Terence Allott, Exeter: University of Exeter Press, 1978.

Hazlitt, William, *Characters of Shakespear's Plays* (1817), *The Complete Works of William Hazlitt*, ed. P. P. Howe, London and Toronto: Dent, 1934, Vol 4.

Huffman, Clifford Chalmers, *Coriolanus in Context*, Lewisburg: Bucknell University Press, 1971.

Jorgensen, Paul A., *Shakespeare's Military World*, Berkeley and Los Angeles: University of California Press, 1956.

Kahn, Coppélia, *Man's Estate: Masculine Identity in Shakespeare*, Berkeley and Los Angeles: University of California Press, 1981.

Kitchin, Laurence, *Mid-Century Drama*, London: Faber &

Faber, 1960, pp. 143–9.

Kitto, H. D. F., *Poiesis: Structure and Thought*, Berkeley and Los Angeles: University of California Press; London: Cambridge University Press, 1966, pp. 355–402.

Knight, G. Wilson, *The Imperial Theme: Further Interpretations of Shakespeare's Tragedies including the Roman Plays*, 3rd edn, London: Methuen, 1951.

Littlewood, J. C. F., 'Coriolanus', *Cambridge Quarterly* 2 (1966–7), pp. 339–57, and 'Coriolanus, II', *Cambridge Quarterly* 3 (1967–8), pp. 28–50.

Long, Michael, *The Unnatural Scene: A Study in Shakespearean Tragedy*, London: Methuen, 1976.

MacCallum, M. W., *Shakespeare's Roman Plays and Their Background*, London: Macmillan, 1910.

Maxwell, J. C., 'Animal Imagery in *Coriolanus*', *Modern Language Review* 42 (1947), pp. 417–21.

————— 'Shakespeare's Roman Plays: 1900–1956', *Shakespeare Survey* 10 (1957), pp. 1–11.

Miola, Robert S., *Shakespeare's Rome*, Cambridge: Cambridge University Press, 1983.

Mulryne, J. R., 'Coriolanus at Stratford-upon-Avon: Three Actors' Remarks', *Shakespeare Quarterly* 29 (1978), pp. 323–32.

Paster, Gail Kern, 'To Starve with Feeding: The City in *Coriolanus*', *Shakespeare Studies* 11 (1978), pp. 123–44.

Phillips, James E. (ed.), *Twentieth Century Interpretations of 'Coriolanus'*, Englewood Cliffs, NJ: Prentice-Hall, 1970.

Rabkin, Norman, *Shakespeare and the Common Understanding*, Chicago and London: University of Chicago Press, 1967.

Rossiter, A. P., *Angel with Horns, and Other Shakespearean Lectures*, ed. Graham Storey, London: Longmans, 1961.

Sanders, Wilbur, and Jacobson, Howard, *Shakespeare's Magnanimity: Four Tragic Heroes, Their Friends and Families*, London: Chatto & Windus, 1978, pp. 136–87.

Sicherman, Carol M., 'Coriolanus: The Failure of Words', *English Literary History* 39 (June 1972), pp. 189–207.

Simmons, J. L., *Shakespeare's Pagan World: The Roman Tragedies*, Charlottesville: University of Virginia Press, 1973; Brighton: Harvester Press, 1974.

Stockholder, Katherine, 'The Other Coriolanus', *PMLA* 85 (1970), pp. 228–36.

Tate, Nahum, *The Ingratitude of a Common-Wealth: Or, the Fall of Caius Martius Coriolanus* (1682), extracts reprinted in Brian Vickers (ed.), *Shakespeare: The Critical Heritage*, vol. I, 1623–1692, London and Boston: Routledge & Kegan Paul, 1974, pp. 386–406.

Tynan, Kenneth, *Tynan on Theatre*, Harmondsworth: Penguin, 1964, pp. 94–6.

Van Dyke, Joyce, 'Making a Scene: Language and Gesture in Coriolanus', *Shakespeare Survey* 30 (1977), pp. 135–46.

Velz, John W., 'The Ancient World in Shakespeare: Authenticity or Anachronism? A Retrospect', *Shakespeare Survey* 31 (1978), pp. 1–12. 'Cracking Strong Curbs Asunder: Roman Destiny and the Roman Hero in Coriolanus', *English Literary Renaissance* 13 (1983), pp. 58–69.

Vickers, Brian, *Shakespeare: Coriolanus*, London: Edward Arnold, 1976.

Willems, Michèle, 'Coriolan ou la parole devaluée', *Travaux de l'Université de Toulouse-Le Mirail*, Série B, Tome 5 (1984), pp. 121–38.

Zeeveld, W. Gordon, 'Coriolanus and Jacobean Politics', *Modern Language Review* 57 (1962), pp. 321–34.

Index

Adelman, Janet 124–5n25, 128n10
Allen, M. J. B. 6, 7

Bacon, Francis 'Of Nature in Men', 'Of Custom and Education' 105–6
Bamber, Linda xviii, 125n25, 130n11, 132n14
Barton, Anne xviii, xix, 122n4, 127n17, 131n8
Bayley, John 32, 49
Berry, Ralph xvi
Bradley, A. C. xix, 6, 111, 120
Brecht, Bertolt xv, 1
Brockbank, Philip xvi, 8, 21, 39, 126n6, n9, 129n26, 131n5, n8
Brower, Reuben xix, 5
Burton, Richard xvi, 69, 71

Calderwood, James L. xx
Camden's Remaines 7
Cantor, Paul A. xix, 53–4, 125n31, 127n16

Chapman, George 64
Charney, Maurice xx, 104, 131n5
Clements, John xvi
Coleridge, Samuel Taylor xviii

Daniell, David xvi
Danson, Lawrence xx, 51–3, 127n19
Dennis, John, The Invader of His Country xv
Dollimore, Jonathan xviii, xix, xx, 122–3n4, 128n6
Doran, Madeleine xx, 123n7

Eagleton, Terry 113
Eliot, T. S. 'Coriolan' 25
Empson, William 17–19, 62–3
Evans, Edith xvi, 69

Fish, Stanley xx

Garrick, David xv, xvi
Glover, Julian 127n20

Goldman, Michael xix, xx,
   123n7, 130n17
Gordon, D. J. xviii, xix,
   126n8
Granville-Barker, Harley 49,
   78, 89, 98, 99, 115
Guinness, Alec xvi
Guthrie, Tyrone xvi, 120

Hall, Joseph, *Characters of
   Vices and Virtues* 126n12
Hall, Peter xvi, 71
Hands, Terry 129n1
Hardy, Alexandre *Coriolan*
   115, 119
Hazlitt, William xviii, 50, 90,
   128n4, 130n14
Heywood, Thomas 64
Hibbard, G. R. 93, 100,
   126n12, 131n5
Hill, Geoffrey 65
Howard, Alan xvi
Huffman, Clifford Chalmers
   xix, 64–5, 127n16

Ibsen, Henrik 14
Irving, Henry xvi

James I, King xix, 64–5
Johnson, Samuel 68
Jones, Emrys 74, 113–14
Jonson, Ben 64
Jorgensen, Paul 126n7

Kahn, Coppélia xviii, 125n25,
   128n10
Kean, Edmund xv, xvi
Kemble, John Philip xv, xvi,
   50
Kipling, Rudyard 58

Kitchin, Laurence xi, xvi–xvii,
   69, 71, 90
Kitto, H. D. F. 6–7, 119, 120
Knight, G. Wilson xx, 131n9
Knights, L. C. 6–7

Littlewood, J. C. F. xviii, 60
Lodge, Thomas 64

McKellen, Ian xvi, 71
Macready, Charles xv, xvi
Machiavelli, Niccolo 106
Maxwell, J. C. 131n9
Miola, R. S. xix, 130n15
Moshinsky, Elijah 98–9,
   125n26
Mulryne, J. R. xvii
Murry, J. Middleton 97–8

Neville, John xvi
North, Thomas *see* Plutarch

Odell, G. C. D. xvii
Olivier, Laurence xi, xvi,
   43–4, 69, 71, 90, 118

Paster, Gail Kern xx, 45–6,
   127n15, 131n9
Phelps, Samuel xvi
Plutarch, 'The Life of Caius
   Martius Coriolanus' 10,
   11–12, 14, 16–17, 28–9,
   39, 43, 44, 56, 82, 84–5,
   88, 89, 99–101, 110

Quayle, Anthony xvi

Rabkin, Norman xviii, xix,
   25–6, 60, 130–1n1
Rossiter, A. P. 59

Sanders, Wilbur xix, 123n4,
  126n5, 130n3
Shakespeare, William
  Antony and Cleopatra xvi,
    37–8, 44
  Cymbeline 65
  Hamlet 8, 51, 78, 111
  Henry IV, Part I 26, 37
  Henry VI, Part I 87
  Julius Caesar 78
  King Lear 63, 78, 80, 104,
    117
  Macbeth 8, 13, 33, 57, 78,
    80, 104, 117
  Othello 8, 30, 44, 78, 111,
    117
  Richard II 35
  Richard III 49
  Romeo and Juliet 78
  Timon of Athens 49, 78
  Titus Andronicus 51–2
  Twelfth Night 38–9
  The Winter's Tale 74–5
Sheridan, Thomas xv
Sicherman, Carol M. xx,
  124n19
Siddons, Sarah xvi
Simmons, J. L. xix, 111–14

Stockholder, Katherine xix,
  129n2

Tate, Nahum, *The Ingratitude
  of a Common-Wealth* xv,
  102, 119
Thomson, James *Coriolanus*
  xv
Thoreau, H. D. 58–9
Thorndike, Sybil xvi
Trilling, Lionel 59–9
Twain, Mark 58
Tynan, Kenneth xvii, 43–4,
  118
Van Dyke, Joyce xx, 126n11
Van Gennep, Arnold 85–6
Vickers, Brian xviii, 59,
  107–8

Walter, John 4
Willems, Michèle 128n8
Williamson, Nicol xvi
Wilson, John Dover 111
Worth, Irene xvi, 125n26
Wrightson, Keith 4

Zeefeld, W. Gordon xix,
  127n16